✳ THE ROAD TO NOW

✳ John Moffitt

THE ROAD
TO NOW

Claiming Our
Spiritual Birthright

Crossroad • New York

1982

The Crossroad Publishing Company
575 Lexington Avenue, New York, NY 10022

Printed in the United States of America

Library of Congress Cataloging in Publication Data

Moffitt, John.
    The road to now.

    Bibliography: p.
    1. Spiritual life—Catholic authors.
2. Moffit, John. I. Title.
BX2350.2.M497   1982   248.2′2   82–4650
ISBN 0–8245–0514–X (pbk.)

✷ CONTENTS

Acknowledgments

Quotations from the Revised Standard Version of the Bible, copyrighted 1946, 1952 © 1971, 1973, are used by permission of the Division of Education and Ministry of the National Council of the Churches of Christ in the U.S.A. Quotations from *The Upanishads,* abridged edition, translated by Swami Nikhilananda, in the 1964 Harper Torchbook edition, © 1963 by George Allen and Unwin, Ltd., are used by permission of Harper & Row, Publishers. Quotations from *The Bhagavad Gita,* translated and with notes by Swami Nikhilananda, © 1944, are used by permission of the Ramakrishna-Vivekananda Center, Inc. The poems "A Warning" and "Seamless Robe," from *This Narrow World,* © 1958 by John Moffitt, are used by permission of Dodd, Mead & Company. "Recognition" and "Presence," from *The Living Seed,* © 1962 by John Moffitt, and "Clear Evening," "At the Spring," and "To See Them," from *Escape of the Leopard,* © 1963, 1966, 1974 by John Moffitt, are used by permission of Harcourt Brace Jovanovich. "A Midday Bath," "A Visit," and "Leap of Vision," from *Signal Message,* © 1982 by John Moffitt, are used by permission of The Golden Quill Press.

✴ PREFACE

T his small and necessarily somewhat personal volume has been six years in the writing. It contains everything I have learned about zeroing in on present actuality. I am painfully aware of my limitations in dealing with so elusive an experience, but I trust that I can offer some insight into what seems to me a matter of vital concern. As lifelong poet and former member of a Hindu monastic order (now returned to his Western roots), I have been concerned almost as far back as I can remember with the problem of how to open oneself, in everyday life, to what the living moment continuously unfolds. My aim here is to help interested readers toward a more conscious living in the Now of things, something I hold to be the birthright of every man and woman. The practical suggestions advanced in these pages originated in my own efforts to claim that birthright for myself.

Those for whom the book is specially designed, and for whom I hope it will have a special appeal, are independent-minded persons who have not found their own truth in any of the existing faiths or philosophies, old or new. It may also prove useful to young people who have had little or no personal contact with either an inherited or adopted religious tradition or a practical philosophy of life, many of whom are undergoing what is nowadays called an "identity crisis." Since it contradicts nothing of the essential witness of any of the great mystical traditions, there is no reason why it should not appeal as well to some who already possess a sufficient faith but who wish to enrich their appreciation and their application of it.

The prologue sets the stage for the four chapters that follow by telling readers not only what they will be reading about but why I think they should read it and how it is designed to help them. The epilogue draws some final conclusions and points to the fruits of achieving full openness to the living moment. Appendix A provides, for the few who may want to live more consistently with their thinking, an outline for devising a flexible routine for daily meditation; Appendix B, a few paragraphs on the various types of gurus or spiritual teachers; Appendix C, a note on mature mystical experience. Additional comments and clarifications, along with sources of quoted material, are listed by page number in the Notes and References.

At various stages in the book's preparation, a great number of friends have given me advice and encouragement. They are too numerous to list in full. But among them are a few—notably Joseph Cunneen, Patrick Hart, ocso, Paul Henry deVries, Ray Staszko, John A. Wheeler, Brian Casey, A. H. Dakin, K. L. S. Rao, and Kenneth W. Morgan—who have examined the entire manuscript and offered useful criticisms and suggestions. I am immensely grateful to all of them, as I am as well to the many I could not name here.

✳ THE ROAD TO NOW

✳ PROLOGUE

A good twenty years ago I learned of a curious incident that has stayed with me ever since. It was told me by a kindly middle-aged couple from Philadelphia, a physician and his wife of substantial means and quite conventional background. They had become concerned about a young man, a recent graduate of an Ivy League college, who was getting treatment in a sanatorium for cirrhosis of the liver. They knew about his illness, they said, because he was the son of good friends of theirs. I gathered that they felt the excessive drinking that had led to his affliction might have come as much from an unfulfilled spiritual need as from a mere physical deficiency. To their knowledge he did not belong to any church or have a settled philosophy of life.

This couple had for some time been studying with a monk of the Ramakrishna Order of India who worked in their city. It occurred to them that his teachings about the self and its intimate relation to God and to the universe might give the young man a fresh slant on life. So they brought him a few pocket-size volumes of lectures delivered by Vivekananda in America in the 1890s. Vivekananda, the first Hindu to restore to modern Indians a pride in their spiritual heritage, founded the order in about 1900. As it happened, the volumes of his lectures were published by a branch of the order, in New York, with which I myself was associated as a monastic member.

The young man became absorbed in reading the books my friends had given him. His malady, however, was further advanced than they realized. Within two weeks they were surprised and saddened to learn that he had succumbed to it. At his funeral they met the nurse who had taken care of him at the sanatorium, and afterwards she told them about his last day.

She had helped him, she said, get out of bed as usual that morning and settle himself in his wheelchair. He then asked her to wheel him to some open French windows that looked out past a low balustrade over the well-kept grounds. It was midmorning and the sun was halfway up the sky. The young man gazed at the sunlit scene. "So it's like this," he said distinctly. Then he was silent. The nurse, who had been straightening up the room, turned to look at him and saw that his head had fallen forward. When she went over to him she found he was dead.

It is possible for anyone with sufficient desire for intuitive understanding to step out of his or her everyday role and see things in a new way—as they are in their nowness. That is the thesis behind this book. Seeing things in their nowness means seeing them with complete attentiveness: in the temporary absence of preoccupations or associations from past or future, there is nothing to distract the senses and the mind from how things truly are. Complete attentiveness in humans implies both self-awareness and awareness of oneself in relation to one's physical and psychological surroundings. To enjoy such an experience means that one is using senses and mind for the first time to full capacity.

Corollary to this thesis is the assumption that to prepare oneself for the experience is to be making the most of one's humanness. Such an exercise is what I call setting out on the Road to Now—the quest for how to zero in on present actuality, how to become fully attentive to all there is to experience in the living moment.

What is said here is said on the basis of a recurring state of mind that I myself have been privileged to enjoy. The awareness it has brought embraces both the immediate environment and the perceiving self, and at the same time a sense of these two in the context of a unifying presence that gives both of them heightened relevance. Looking back on my several experiences of this state, I feel that I have enjoyed the incursion, as it were, of creatively working spirit along with a sense of participation in its working. The experiences to date have not been, I realize, protracted enough to have had the transforming impact of a profound mystical realization. Still, they have given me sufficient firsthand knowledge to make it seem worthwhile to share the experience with others.

It was to bolster my assertion that it is possible to step out of one's everyday role and see things in a new way that I began this prologue with the story of the young man and what he said at the point of death. What he experienced, I suspect, was something even more decisively transforming than the state of mind I have described. The fact that he obtained it seemingly without preparation helps clarify our understanding of it. Most mystics have undergone a long and arduous course of preparation before attaining spiritual insight. When all is said and done, however, it is generally agreed that such an experience comes only through the grace of circumstances beyond one's control. From what the young man had read, and because of what he had suffered, his mind had evidently become open to the Now of things without his having made a conscious effort. Had he lived longer, perhaps he would have made further efforts to refine his attentiveness.

In my own case, the experience I enjoyed allowed me on its first occurrence to step out of my everyday role for the better part of two days. As a direct result, my alertness to and participation in whatever of my surroundings offered itself in any one moment was noticeably enhanced. A new dimension of being revealed itself. When the experience passed it was only natural to try to reawaken it and perhaps to intensify it. I soon found, however, that no amount of effort on my part had any effect. The state has since recurred on several occasions, as I have indicated, but always completely unexpectedly.

Finally it occurred to me that though I myself could do nothing to ensure its return, I could at least *invite* a similar occurrence by reproducing the conditions that accompanied it, namely, the intense attentiveness toward everything I perceived without and within. I realized, of course, that it is impossible for anyone to be attentive to the whole of one's surroundings in all their detail simply by willing oneself to be so. What one must devise is a means to *persuade* the mind to be attentive. It seems obvious that the mind concentrates far more easily on something or someone that fascinates it than on something or someone it has to force itself to concentrate on. I was fortunate enough to hit upon a plan that took these facts into account. To a certain extent this book follows the order of my attempts to persuade my own mind into a proper attitude of openness to things as they are.

The same course of action is not only possible but readily available to anyone with sufficient desire. I say this because there is probably no human being, except the mentally deficient, who lacks the capacity for attentiveness. All of us, even if simply for self-preservation, have had to turn full attention to some job we were doing, some conversation we were carrying on, some train of thought we were following—no matter how briefly. Most of us, too, have experienced something beyond such examples of willed attentiveness. Who among us cannot recall unexpected moments of attentiveness so complete that there has been no sense of outer or inner, of a perceiving "me" or a perceived object or "you"? Such experiences can come during undistracted enjoyment of natural beauty, in hearing music or reading poetry, in giving and accepting love. They occur, too, during periods of activity—while we engage in creative work, in research, or in competitive sports. They involve an awareness deeply open to the immediate object of perception.

In such vivid moments, which we look back upon as moments of flawless satisfaction, the experience is of an undivided wholeness. There is a fusing, as it were, of the inner perceiver and the object perceived. It occurs as well in moments of physical pain or mental anguish: where we can be objective enough we find in these as well evidence of the very same sort of fusing. Once we are possessed of sufficient desire to see into the Now of things, we are thus assured of being already gifted with the necessary tool for preparing the proper conditions for openness to the living moment. But the dimension of being such openness reveals goes beyond the sorts of attentiveness just mentioned.

Those persons fortunate enough to have already experienced a passing sense of the Now of things are aware that it involves an even more intense and continuous attentiveness. Different from the heightened consciousness that some persons occasionally obtain through meditation or prayer, it consists in being fully open to the immediate context of perception, which in this case is the totality of one's immediate surroundings. Nothing dazzling, it wields instead a gentle persuasiveness that becomes elusive as soon as it is thought about analytically. A childlike yet surprisingly down-to-earth state of mind, it is convincing enough to leave no doubt about its authenticity. Once again, the experience is of an undivided wholeness, but it does not entail so radical a fusing of the outer or inner world and the perceiver that they become indistinguishable. The sense of inner perceiver and perceived world is not lost. Instead, both are embraced in a unifying presence that shows them in a new light. Those who share such periods of insight (usually considerably longer than the moments of intense but "fused" attentiveness mentioned earlier) become irrefutably convinced through personal witness that they are seeing things as they really are.

As already noted, the plan I devised to invite a return of the desired awareness of the Now of things was not to force but to persuade the mind to give devoted attention to the world around me and the world within. To attract its attention to the outer aspect of my surroundings, the knowable world of matter outside me, I took what I felt to be the most arresting symbol of it and began directing my attention to it. That symbol was—and is—the sun. I found it to be exceedingly useful as a symbol because, once adopted as an object of contemplation, by its very nature it *compels* attentiveness. Without it the earth could not have come into being, the human race could not have evolved, and without it I myself could not continue to be. Thinking of how indispensable it is to us, and reminding myself of its more important characteristics, I found that it was becoming for me a central presence. As a result, the direction of my thinking about my outer environment began to change. I developed a new awareness of the meaning and immense value of all the living and nonliving things dependent on the sun. Along with this awareness came a spontaneous attentiveness to all of them as they came to my notice.

To attract the mind to the inner aspect of my surroundings, the world of thought and feeling within me, I again took what I felt to be its most arresting symbol and began by directing my attention to it. That symbol was—and is—that inexhaustible source of energy, the self. Once recognized for what it is, the self becomes useful as a symbol, because it also compels attention quite as much as does the sun. By my *self* I understand not the ego-self or any of the other aspects of the human person, but my core experience, the true *I* in which there is no identification with body or mind. Without the self there would be no awareness for me of either the world outside me or the world within. Thinking of how indispensable it is to me and to all other persons, and reminding myself when necessary of what it is not, I found that, just as with the sun, it was becoming for me a central presence. The direction of my thinking about my inner environment, the psychological world within, likewise began to change. I developed a new awareness of the meaning and immense value of the multitudinous world of the self, and equally of all the other selves I encountered in the course of each day. Along with it came a more spontaneous attentiveness to the various details of the inner world as I was faced with them, and more particularly to all the posturings of the ego-self with which I habitually, but mistakenly, identified myself.

I have not yet come anywhere near complete success in my efforts at continuous attentiveness to the outer and inner worlds through contemplation of the sun and the self. But perhaps by chance, perhaps through attentiveness to these two symbols themselves, I have occasionally enjoyed brief recurrences of the sense of creatively working spirit. I came to see that it is indeed spirit that joins the two worlds, in my most intense moments, into one undivided whole. Because of this function, I concluded, the world of spirit thought of as a separate entity should be regarded as a third aspect of the environment that surrounds me and therefore should receive my attention along with its two counterparts.

But attentiveness to the world of spirit needed a different approach, if the mind was to be persuaded toward it, from that used for the world of the sun or the world of the self. There can be no symbol for the world of spirit: spirit and its world are in reality one and the same. One needs, therefore, to concentrate on creative spirit itself, which is continuously offering itself to our awareness. To help make it real to myself I found I did better to think *around* it rather than about it.

The first three chapters of this book are devoted to these three aspects of the human environment. The first chapter leads the mind toward greater at-homeness with the sun and what it stands for, by acquainting readers who may have neglected it with its reality as an immediate presence. To help make it vividly real, I explore what I myself and then what others—ancient sun worshipers as well as modern astrophysicists—have observed or experienced in encounters with the sun. I also consider what results anyone may expect from a similar encounter. "The Now of the Sun," this chapter's title, refers to the immediate whole of the world for which the sun stands as symbol. It reminds us, as well, that the sun is an integral part of our nowness: both as symbol and in itself, it is always present to us and to all earthly things. It is vital to our own and our physical environment's being and survival.

The second chapter leads the mind toward greater at-homeness with the self and what it stands for, by acquainting readers who have neglected it with its reality as an immediate presence. Being knowable only through intuition, the self is not easily identified. A different procedure is required from that used in the first chapter. Starting from my own and others' observations and experiences of the world of the self, the inner world, it gradually narrows its sights on what the true *I* means to each of us. In this way the self, too, should become vividly real. Only then do we deal directly with the self and consider some of the results anyone may expect from an encounter with it. "The Now of the Self," this chapter's title, refers to the immediate whole of the inner world for which the self stands as symbol. It reminds us, as well, that the self is an integral part of our nowness: both as symbol and in itself, the true *I* (whether recognized or ignored) is always present to our inner world—even in dreams or dreamless states, as is attested by memory—and to our vision of the outer world. It is as vital to our own and our subjective world's being and survival as the sun is to the objective world.

The third chapter leads the mind toward greater at-homeness with the intuition of spirit by seeking to refine and intensify readers' sense of its presence. To help make it more vividly real, I explore first my own observation and experience of spirit, and then those of others. Finally I consider in some detail its working all about us and in every depth within us. "The Now of Spirit," this chapter's title, refers to the immediateness of the creative process that weaves, as it were, our environment, outer and inner, into one seamless whole—the whole that even now we sometimes experience it to be. It refers to that presence thought of as *pervadingly at work,* and not as a separate agent "between" the other two aspects of the environment. It reminds us that spirit is the essence of the Now of things, and therefore that it is always present to all material and mental phenomena.

To have become so well acquainted with the three aspects of our environment—our physical, psychic, and spiritual surroundings—that we feel intellectually and emotionally at home with them is, however, only the preliminary stage of our journey on the Road to Now. Continuous though relaxed effort is necessary if we are to become fully prepared for the awareness that participates in the moment that is now—allowing us to step out of our everyday role and see things as they are. The fourth chapter of the book, "The Road to Now," outlines some regular practices that I myself try to follow so as to be more continuously attentive during the course of the day to the symbols chosen for the world of the sun and the world of the self, and to the spirit that in times of penetrating insight we see as weaving the two worlds into the whole they really are. It is my hope that the practices may be of benefit to some others possessed of a sufficient desire. To encourage further effort, this chapter also mentions what we may expect as a result of our receiving the awareness we have been seeking.

This book's aim, then, is to help readers function up to full capacity as humans and so make themselves worthy of the transforming insight that would make of them complete human beings. Reading it is not enough. To enter upon the Road to Now in earnest means more than informing oneself about how to train the intellect and the emotions to fix on symbols. It means becoming so intimately at home with these symbols and their worlds that, when the time is ripe, attentiveness to them comes spontaneously, without the tension that goes with an ego-prompted drive for fulfillment.

✳ THE NOW OF THE SUN

A WARNING

Do not look at the sun
When, naked and remote,
It rides the middle skies—
A core of churning flame
Whose incandescent glare
Obliterates the sight
Of every other thing
For him who looks at it
Too intently and too long—
Lest, seeing, you should see,
Lest the immensity
Should enter through your eyes
And suffer you no more
To dream convenient lies.
But look, instead, at the glow
Its flaming disk assumes
At sundown or at dawn,
And, like a modest snail,
Cower in comfort here
Inside this world's blue shell,
Not venturing beyond
To any bleaker sphere
Where grace does not abound.
Before the fear dispels,
Before the threat is gone,
Turn away your eyes
From the elemental blaze.
Turn away from the sun.

When I was a boy I often took it into my head to stare at the sun directly. I found that if I looked long enough, till my eyes stopped watering, I observed a strange phenomenon. I saw in the center of the flaming mass a dark area with something like the rich clarity of molten gold under a blowtorch. Perhaps it was an illusion caused by the dazzling brightness all around it, but it seemed to me I was in touch with something hidden from ordinary sight, something more central than the light. On turning away from it, of course, I saw nothing but small suns wherever I looked. At the time I spoke of my habit to no one. Several friends have told me recently that in childhood they, too, sometimes looked at the sun, though not for so many seconds at a time. (One is especially warned nowadays against looking at the sun during an eclipse. It is risky, however, to do so at any time. No one should expose the eyes to it in any way that might harm the delicate tissues of the retina. Why no injury was done to mine I cannot say.)

After those early days sometimes I looked directly at the sun, but I never made it a regular practice. Yet the very urge to make contact with the innermost secret of the sun, as revealed in that early behavior, indicates a healthy instinct to keep as close to one's natural surroundings—celestial as well as earthly—as one can. To be sure, the original urge of childhood was crowded out in the end by more sophisticated concerns. Yet the poem quoted at the start of this chapter, which I wrote many years later, echoes that early experience. Though it warns—with conscious irony— *not* to stare at the sun if one wants to live in "comfort," it still betrays a lingering fascination with what I had seen.

There have been occasions since boyhood when the sun has forced itself on my awareness. I recall a near total eclipse that took place one summer when I was about fifteen years old. The sun cast small moon-shaped images on the ground through the leaves as the eclipse moved nearer and nearer to its highest point. Birds began twittering in the trees as if they were going to roost. A preternatural darkness pervaded the air. All these phenomena were impressive enough. But what struck me most forcefully was the unexpected appearance of some of the brighter stars. I was suddenly reminded, at midday, of the measureless abyss of star-strewn space that enfolds our solar system. The sun was showing itself for what it really was: a living star in a vast concourse of living stars. Our place in the cosmos—which I, for one, habitually forgot—had for the moment become a cause for wonder. Why did I live out my daytimes as if that vastness of space did not exist?

More recently I noted what seemed to me the impatience and even embarrassment of adult men and women in New York City at having to confront the fact of the sun. During a partial eclipse I was walking up Fifth Avenue through the considerably darkened afternoon. Reverting to my boyhood habit, I briefly looked straight at the sun and easily made out the great bite the moon had taken out of its disk. But as I passed people on the sidewalk, I felt that most of them wanted to be doggedly about their business (as all sensible, practical people should be wanting, no doubt). The phenomenon would soon cease, and they simply ignored what was going on in the sky. Only one small group of teenagers, sitting on the wide steps of Saint Patrick's Cathedral, were using a card with a pinhole in it to cast the image of the sun's crescent onto another card. How these particular young people felt about the sun I could not know. At least they were not indifferent to what was going on around them in their outer environment. And certainly the fact of the eclipse did not irk or embarrass them at all. I could not help thinking how much all the rest were missing.

When we open ourselves sufficiently to the sun's near presence, we see it as a potent reality. It becomes for us a stepping-off place into a universe of all-encompassing and unimaginably boundless matter and space. It becomes, too, our best means of introduction to everything immediately around us that derives from it. Was this not what my own mind was trying to tell me when in childhood I stared directly at the sun? However that may be, in the past several years I myself have felt a strong urge to renew my earlier intimacy with it. And the result is a fresh sense of relatedness to the myriad objects—near and far, great and small—of the physical world about me. I now make it a practice to glance indirectly, and very briefly, at the sun whenever the opportunity offers itself.

* * *

When we think about our spiritual evolution as humans, we cannot help being struck by the importance that early man gave to the sun. From the findings of archaeologists we learn that very many, perhaps all, of the peoples of antiquity believed that through it a living creative power was to be known. The first to give eloquent literary expression to their feelings about the sun were the Egyptians.

Throughout Egypt's history, even from before the time of the First Dynasty, which began about 3100 B.C., the sun had been an object of daily ritual worship. In the fourteenth century B.C. a superb hymn of grateful adoration of the solar orb, the Aton, was composed. The "Hymn to the Aton" was inscribed on the walls of the intended tomb at Tell el Amarna of Pharaoh Akhnaton's personal scribe and commander of horse, the "Divine Father" Ay. (After serving as vizier to the youthful Tutankhamon, he himself became pharaoh for a few years.) We are indebted to Akhnaton, tenth pharaoh of the Eighteenth Dynasty, for the inspiration and no doubt most of the wording of this masterpiece.

HYMN TO THE ATON

O living Aton, source and begetter of life,
Fair is your rising on the world's rim:
When you dawn in the east you flood every land with
　your splendor . . .
For you are Re: you reach their limits and seize them
　for your dear Son.
Remote though you dwell, your rays shower down upon earth;
You rest within sight of men, yet to them your ways
　are hidden.

When you set, on the edge of the West,
The earth is wrapped in a darkness as of death;
Men pass the night inside their houses,
Their heads wrapped up, not seeing one another . . .
When you rise on the Eastward rim and dazzle forth

As orb of the sun, the earth grows light . . .
Trees and plants grow greener, birds fly from their nests,
Their wings lifted in praise of your Spirit.
All animals leap and play . . .
Every way opens at your dawning.
The fishes in the Great River sport in your presence,
Your rays are in the midst of the sea.

It is you who cause women to conceive, who make the seed
    to become a man,
You who give life to the child in the womb,
Who comfort it so that it does not cry there,
Nurse that you are, even in the womb . . .
When the chick chirps inside the shell, you give him breath
    to sustain him,
You appoint for him the right period within the egg
So that he may pierce the shell and come out . . .

How varied your works are! They are hidden from men's
    sight,
O sole God, like to whom there is no other.
When you rested alone, you fashioned this earth to your
    wish—
All men, all cattle great and small,
All creatures that move on the face of the earth . . .
You create the waters under the earth
And bring them forth, as you will, to support the people
    of Egypt . . .
All far-off, alien lands as well—for them you sustain
    their life:
For them you have placed another River in the sky
To flow forth and cause a flood to descend on the
    mountains, like a sea,
To water the fields of their villages . . .

Millions of forms you have created out of yourself:
Towns, villages, fields, roads, the Great River.

All eyes behold you before them,
For you are the Aton of Day, high above all you have created.

You live, O God, in my heart, but there is none other
Who knows you truly but your Son, Akhnaton.
Him you have made wise in your designs and your power.

This late poetic flowering of a tradition of sun worship that had continued in Egypt from predynastic times is well worth studying in its entirety. I have shortened it here and shorn it of much colorful detail. For anyone who knows the art of this period, the picture that immediately rises in the mind when reading these words is the solar orb with down-reaching rays ending in a life-giving, creative hand.

In the "Hymn to the Aton" occurs one of the first hints, in the religious traditions that have directly influenced the West, of a sole God—even a Father—who constantly toils for the good of his creatures and with whom worshipers can enjoy personal intimacy in the heart. True, Pharaoh Akhnaton and his queen, Nefertiti, embodiments of the sun, were the only persons who directly worshiped the Aton. Others, whether aristocrats or commoners, received their blessing by looking upon and venerating them. But the idea of deity that Akhnaton offered them must have been more appealing to imaginative minds, however obedient they may have been by habit to royal decree, than the idea served by the former royal priesthood of Amon, the "Hidden One," whose worship had for long years been the state religion. One senses in the pictured scenes of Akhnaton's court a spontaneity not found in earlier representations of royal life in Egypt. It may well be, as has been suggested, that the pharaoh was actually resuscitating an ancient tradition of solar worship, not introducing an utterly original teaching. Yet obviously something fresh and exhilarating had been added to whatever he had revived from antiquity. It was perhaps largely because of his fanatical suppression, near the end of his reign, of all the popular gods that the people became restive. Nobles and commoners alike evidently responded to a call for a return to worship of Amon.

And so the new and less mysterious religion endured only till the pharaoh's death—a period of no more than seventeen years.

Quite possibly about the same time that Akhnaton was conceiving the subtle expressions of the "Hymn to the Aton," an Indo-Aryan sage first uttered by the Ganges River what has become the most sacred verse of the Hindu scriptures, the Vedas. An invocation to the sun, it is called the Gayatri Mantra and is repeated even today by millions of Hindus, both sophisticated and uneducated, in their daily devotions:

> We meditate on the unsurpassed
> splendor of Savitr, the divine vivifier:
> may he stimulate our understanding.

This verse, which appears in the Rig-Veda, about the fourteenth century B.C., belongs to a tradition of sun worship in India that had already existed at least a thousand years.

Evidence of sun worship has been found in India from Neolithic times, and representations of it occur on seals and pottery from the Indus Valley civilization. But it is in the early Vedic age that we have literary evidence of such worship. Among a number of aspects of the sun, at least two attained great importance. Surya, the dispeller of darkness, is the shining orb visible in the heavens, described as "celestial, well-winged, swift-moving, and majestic" and as "the beholder of good and bad deeds." He is sometimes pictured as an eagle. Savitr, the aspect invoked in the Gayatri Mantra just quoted, denotes the sun's more abstract qualities as "stimulator, instigator, impeller, animator of all"—in a word, its quickening aspect. He is described as being the power behind the visible Surya. Both are described as golden haired, and Savitr is said to have eyes, hands, tongue, and arms of gold, to wear golden armor, and to travel in a golden chariot drawn by white horses.

Sometimes Surya and Savitr are identified in the Rig-Veda, but usually their functions are sharply distinguished. An ancient commentator on the Vedas states that Savitr is the sun before it rises and Surya the sun between sunrise and sunset. There is a certain resemblance between these two and the Egyptian gods Amon (the "Hidden One") and Aton (the visible solar orb). In the Rig-Veda, the sun-god conceived as the creative power is often called the supreme god and identified with the Supreme Spirit.

There are innumerable other references to the sun in Hindu sacred literature. In forest retreats in India, some seven or eight centuries after the Rig-Veda's text achieved its final form, poet-sages spoke of the sun. In a passage in one of the earliest of their mystical treatises, the sun is equated with Satya, the True, who is ultimate reality. The sage seems to go beyond Akhnaton in directing attention to the "being in the sun" rather than to the visible orb of the sun (though, as we saw, the concept of a reality —the "Hidden One"—behind the visible sun was already present in Egyptian religious thinking). And in another early treatise, composed about the same time, occurs a striking prayer to be repeated by someone at the point of death:

> The door of the Truth is covered by a golden disk.
> Open it, O Nourisher!
> Lift it away so that I who have been worshiping
> Truth may behold it.
> O Nourisher, lone traveler of the sky!
> Controller!
> O Sun, offspring of Prajapati, Lord of Creation!
> Gather your rays, withdraw your light.
> I would see, through your grace,
> That form of yours which is the fairest.
> I am indeed he, that Supreme Person, who dwells there.

Here is recognition that the sun is not only the source of life, but a person with whom one can establish a prayer relationship and through whom the worshiper can, by his grace, realize his own true identity. The sun provides a means for the worshiper to go beyond it to a higher reality, which, however, is not separate from the identity of the sun.

Many later references to the sun as a divine power bear witness to the importance of sun worship in India. And such worship, as I mentioned, has persisted among Hindus on all levels of society to the present day. The sun has always been held there to be one of the chief symbols of ultimate reality.

Formal sun worship was not confined to Egypt and India. It was passed down to later cultures. Assyria, Babylonia, Persia, Greece, and Rome venerated the sun in varying degree. Its worship is found also in numerous places in the New World. Like the ancient Britons who constructed the immense observatory at Stonehenge, Mayan astronomer-architects in about 500 B.C. designed and erected temples in Mesoamerica positioned to mark the cycles of sun and moon. These massive structures point to some form of sun worship as surely as does the imposing temple of Amon-Re at Karnak, built a thousand years earlier in Egypt by pharaohs of the Eighteenth Dynasty. It now appears that Iberian Celts, perhaps even earlier than the Mayans, introduced sun worship into North America, especially New England, sometime around 800 B.C. The long axes of the larger of their modest temple-observatories are so aligned as to point directly to the rising sun at the winter and summer solstices: it could be observed from the altar only on the three or four days around those times.

Here is a Celtic hymn to the sun, perhaps known by these early colonists:

> The eye of the great god,
> The eye of the god of glory,
> The eye of the king of hosts,
> The eye of the king of life,
> Shining upon us through time and tide,
> Shining upon us gently and without stint.
>
> Glory to thee, O splendid Sun,
> Glory to thee, O Sun, face of the god
>   of life.

In Central and South America, besides the Maya, many other cultures—Olmec, Toltec, Aztec, Inca—acknowledged the sun's divinity. Sun worship was flourishing among the Aztecs when the Spaniards found and despoiled them in the sixteenth century.

And this same tradition is preserved today among the Pueblo peoples in Arizona and New Mexico.

Coincidentally, just about the time I began to be aware of a spiritual element in my own relationship with the sun, I came to know the family of a Hopi Antelope Chief in Arizona. On one of my several visits to their village on the Second Mesa, I had a talk with a son of this chief, himself a priest of the same society. Knowing how closely bound up with the sun their religious tradition is, I mentioned to him how important the sun was to me. He gave me a piercing look. "The sun is our God," he said with great earnestness. In reply to a further question he acknowledged also (if I understood him correctly) that there is a Creative Power beyond the physical sun. I did not gather, however, that one could have a personal relationship with the Creator. Could this Power not be closely related to Tloque Nahuaque, the God of the Aztec poet-king Nezahualcoyotl, whom he worshiped in his heart as Creator—he, the one ruler who could not endure human sacrifice and did not partake in it? This is how he invoked him:

> Lord of the Close Vicinity,
> Lord of the With and the By,
> The Ever Present,
> The god who demands no sacrifices,
> Who is the Twofold Lord and the Twofold Lady,
> Lord of our Subsistence,
> Lord of Creation, god of night and wind,
> Invisible and without form.

Perhaps the Hopis had forgotten this hidden aspect of God. Or perhaps it was not appropriate for my friend to talk about it.

Among the Hebrews, too, the sun appears to have claimed a certain amount of attention. In several of the psalms there are striking references to it. A few of the characteristics of the sun poetically described in Akhnaton's "Hymn to the Aton" are close enough to those of Yahweh as found in Psalm 104 to have prompted the conjecture that the hymn was the source of certain lines of that particular psalm. It has even been suggested that

Akhnaton's ideas about the sun as sole God may have helped the Hebrews shape their concept of deity.

But there never was in Judaism any identification of the sun with God. This is also true, of course, of Christianity and Islam. As a result of the revelations of prophets and other scriptural writers, all three religions instilled in their followers a belief in a God who created all things, including the sun. Significantly, what Christianity succeeded in doing was to place another sun, the "Sun of Righteousness," before its believers. It was that sun, of which Saint John speaks at the beginning of his Gospel, who provided the "true light that enlightens every man."

What we see, then, is that at a certain turning point in history a culture that for tens of centuries would be a major force in world civilization took up the concept of a transcendent deity and left it to others in the East and in Mesoamerica to preserve the age-old belief in the sun itself as a source of creative power and spiritual inspiration.

Reminders of the ancient way of believing have continued to echo from time to time in Christian tradition. In Saint Francis of Assisi's well-known "Canticle of the Sun" occur the lines:

> Praised be my Lord God with all his creatures,
> and especially our brother the sun,
> who brings us the day and who brings us the night;
> fair is he and shines with a very great splendor.
> O Lord, he signifies you to us.

(In fact, the whole canticle is a paean of praise for the visible creation, the element of our environment that we are thinking about in this chapter.) And in one of the verses of John Wesley's famous hymn, "Hark! the Herald Angels Sing," we even find a hint of the Egyptian image of the sun as a winged orb:

> Hail the heaven-born Prince of Peace!
> Hail the Sun of righteousness!
> Light and life to all he brings,
> Risen with healing in his wings.

But the sun, which from time immemorial in the old civilizations had taken hold of the human heart and claimed its awe and wonder, was no longer seen by the vast majority in the West as a source of spiritual inspiration. It would be left to others, not generally thought to be capable of exerting a religious influence, to encourage men and women to turn their attention back to this living star, the immediate source of their being and life, and of their continued evolution.

* * *

It is a commonplace today that the sun is the center of the solar system, a fact unknown in Europe till about the sixteenth century. The revolutionary discoveries of Copernicus and Galileo opened the way for modern astronomers not only to make estimates about the movements of the planets around the sun, but finally to construct theories about the sun's internal makeup and about how the planets came into being. But it is only in the past several decades that their discoveries about the universe have captured the imagination of people outside the observatory or the classroom—largely through the writings of several gifted astronomers. Even so, few of us today know as much as we might about the findings of modern astronomers and the speculations of astrophysicists regarding this source of energy in our near neighborhood.

No scientific theory about the sun's nature, of course, need be accepted as an unassailable statement of fact. But it is useful to review briefly some of the scientists' conclusions. The theories they have constructed are based not on guesswork but on responsible assessment of scientifically determined facts. And we cannot familiarize ourselves with the sun, and come to a sense of our own personal relation to it, without knowing the gist of what the best scientific speculation, firmly based on painstaking observation, has to say about it.

According to the estimates of astrophysicists, the sun has existed in its present state for some five billion years. What has kept this tremendous mass of incandescent matter—864,000 miles in diameter and weighing more than 330,000 times as much as the earth—in a more or less stable condition over such an extended period of time?

One modern theory goes like this: The sun is known to be composed of two gases—hydrogen and a lesser amount of helium. Even on its surface their temperature reaches over 5,500 degrees Celsius (10,000 degrees Fahrenheit)—and that of the solar flares associated with sunspots is thousands of times higher. (It is helpful to remember that what we, in human terms, call "heat" is, in terms of the sun, atomic excitement.) At its core, owing to the tremendous weight of the sun's whole mass exerted through force of gravity, the temperature is higher still. And yet, despite the pressure exerted on the gases at the core, the sun has not collapsed. The reason is that in the period during which it has existed in its present state, the core has been surrounded by layers of condensed and very hot gas. Each of these layers in turn exerts sufficient pressure outward to keep it from collapsing under the weight of the layers outside it.

But what is the sun's inner temperature, and what explains its continuous outflow of heat?

Knowing the amount of intermixed hydrogen and helium in the sun, and the surface temperature, astrophysicists at several research centers figured out the density and temperature of each of the layers—estimating the mass of each in such a way as not to exceed or fall short of the total mass. When in their figurings they reached the central core, they arrived at a startling result. The temperature at the core, they concluded, should be roughly 21,110,000 degrees Celsius (38,000,000 degrees Fahrenheit). This is the approximate temperature at which, it has been found, the nuclei of hydrogen atoms in a reactor begin to fuse—just what happens when a hydrogen bomb is exploded.

At the sun's core there is thus a continuous process of transformation in which the nuclei of hydrogen atoms, unimaginable numbers of them, are forced together at an umimaginably high temperature (or rate of excitation). The product of this fusion is ultimately helium gas. At the same time, as a direct result of the forming of heavier nuclei from the particles making up the hydrogen nuclei, there is a release of energy in the form of "flashes" of radiation—the very same energy that held together the original hydrogen atoms. But unlike what happens in the exploding of a hydrogen bomb, the layers of gas enclosing the sun's core are able to contain the explosion and thus the temperature is maintained at just the intensity needed for the nuclei to continue to fuse. The energy released as the helium is formed penetrates through the enveloping layers and escapes from the sun's surface as light and heat and cosmic rays. But the journey from core to surface is by no means a speedy one. For the escaping radiant energy to reach the surface it may require a few million years—a statement that is more understandable when we learn that a hydrogen atom has been estimated to be one 250-millionth of an inch in diameter.

This is a highly simplified summary of some of the best scientific thinking on the subject. There are other theories, but all maintain that the source of the sun's energy is very likely the fusion of hydrogen-atom nuclei at the sun's core.

The sun, we are told, is a minor star near the edge of our galaxy of some 100 billion live stars. Even so its mass is for us almost inconceivable. Two million tons of matter, it has been estimated, are turned into radiation at the surface and escape each second. And a single solar flare, which may last up to thirty minutes, can give off one thousandth of the total presently available energy of the sun from an area of the surface that is no more than one ten-thousandth of its whole area. Yet the supply of close-pressed hydrogen is sufficient to last for another five billion years. Before its present state alters, the sun will have remained roughly the same for a period of ten billion years—after this time the outer layers will begin to expand. It will then continue to exist, so the theory goes, as a body known as a "red giant," one hundred times its present size, for something like 100 million years more.

How the sun became the atomic furnace it is and how the nine planets came to circle round it has been variously explained. According to one theory, the original solar matter formed a vast cloud, or nebula, of gas and dust at least as large as the entire solar system today—ninety-nine percent of it hydrogen and helium. The cloud was cool in the beginning; but within some millions of years the center of the mass, because of its growing concentration through agglomeration of particles and through gravity, began to grow hotter. Gradually the heavier elements in the cloud, the one percent that was not hydrogen or helium, collected into secondary concentrations of denser matter wheeling about the increasingly hot central core. These heavier elements, such as silicon and the various metals, along with carbon, nitrogen, and oxygen, formed compounds among themselves and with some of the hydrogen. As the core of the sun became critically hot, the expanding pressure of the radiation swept all the lighter material out into space, leaving the larger concentrations of the heavier elements and their compounds in orbit. These drew to themselves whatever elements remained around them, and thus slowly formed the planets, whose composition is radically different from that of the sun. Meanwhile the outer reaches of the central cloud of gas had formed into the layers already mentioned and insured that the fusion at the center would go on uninterruptedly.

Just how the cloud of gas found itself in this particular location in the galaxy and how the heavier elements joined it, we need not ask. I have described the formation of the sun and the planets simply to help our minds feel at home in the physical universe. Further refinements of the theory will hardly serve our purpose. It would be tempting to find a parallel in Hindu cosmogony to the "big bang" theory of the deploying of the observable cosmos perhaps thirteen billion years ago—noting that this theory requires an endless series of expansions and subsequent contractions. But we may leave such speculation to better qualified minds and confine our thinking to our immediate surroundings. This much we may confidently say: modern astrophysicists have substantiated the ancients' belief that the sun itself is a showing forth of elemental creative power.

* * *

Our prehistoric ancestors' worship of the sun as a deity was not entirely the result of superstition. Given their situation it was almost inevitable that they should worship it. Their day's activities began with the blazing up of the sun's orb at dawn and ended with its disappearance at dusk—as they do still for traditionalist Hopis and members of other Pueblo tribes. When, at the winter solstice, the sun in northern regions seemed on its way to sinking past recovery, perhaps at first they felt they had to help it return with prayers and chants and ceremonies. Later, when they understood things better, they used its observable recurrent behavior to regulate planting and harvesting. It would have been then, no doubt, that their ceremonies became celebrations.

These ancestors of ours could hardly forget what they owed to the sun. As its heat intensified with spring and summer, life in temperate climates became less of a struggle. Food gatherers could find more abundant roots and vegetables, seeds and fruits and nuts. As experience gradually taught them, they could grow crops. Even in tropical climates the sun's vital role was understood when, after a flood or monsoon, farmers could once more raise and harvest grain and edible plants. Their worship would have sprung from their knowledge of where their life and strength originated. They may at times have feared the source of their life and strength, but except in periods of drought the sun would surely have seemed more benign than gods of storm and lightning and thunder and wind and earthquake. Possibly it was out of the ancients' reverence for the sun and their gratitude to it that some of the important elements of religion as we now know it were born.

As we look at the history of religion, it may seem strange that one large segment of humanity—the Near Eastern and European —was able to put the sun out of their religious thinking. Just why they turned away from it so completely need not concern us today. Yet we do well to ask whether, in the light of the consequences, they really should have turned so far away. In transferring their allegiance to the transcendent reality revealed in the great Semitic traditions, were they justified in all but banishing the sun from their religious consciousness? Have the Hindus and the Hopis, to mention only two groups, been able to keep in closer touch with their natural environment than we have, just because they have *not* completely turned away from it?

In arriving at our belief in a God transcending the visible sun, we modern Westerners and Near Easterners have lost sight of the rather obvious fact that the sun is not unrelated to the divine. In its own way, as the immediate source of all the elemental cosmic energy directly knowable to humans apart from a faith or profound mystical experience, it is (as astrophysicists are demonstrating) a clear showing forth of creative power. In turning away from it, we have effectively withdrawn our reverence and gratitude from the immediate source of the long series of achievements—physical and mental and spiritual—of humankind on a sun-washed, sun-fed, almost sun-created planet. By denying it our appreciation and worship we have maimed our spirituality, as any cutting off of oneself from one's roots must do. What is more, we have laid ourselves open to a potent danger.

Our Western and Near Eastern religions in their present form rely, except for the sometimes distrusted witness of mystics, on a faith in God based on revelation and understood through religious myths and dogmas. The dogmas developed—under the inspiration, it was believed, of the Holy Spirit or some similar principle—from what had been revealed about God through scripture. That they developed under divine inspiration was itself accepted on the basis of statements in scripture and, among Christians, the word of the early Church Fathers.

Human nature has a tendency to seek out what it sees as the most congenial route to its goals. To seek a more demanding way requires exercise of will. Unimaginative and uninquisitive minds often turn to such an organized body of teaching in any field as a comfortable refuge from the effort required for creative thought based on personal experience. Instead of finding in the teaching a source of inspiration for individual adventure and discovery, they make it into a matter for routine intellectual or emotional allegiance.

This is what appears to have happened to much religious thinking in the West and the Near East. The transcendent God toward whom the Judeo-Christian revelation pointed the Western world has for very many people become walled about with concepts and symbols taken at second hand. Certainly all of these have originally accompanied direct experience and as such merit respect, but they are not in themselves experience. In causing many of us to lose sight of what is beyond thought and feeling and speech, they have caused us to lose sight of our total meaning as humans.

Several sources of information are available to us about how we may profit more meaningfully from the myths and dogmas of revelation, and so reassert our humanity. The first of these is the testimony of true gurus, or spiritual guides. These are the mystics and saints—and perhaps a few extraordinary artists, poets, philosophers, psychoanalysts, theologians. Yet such unique spirits are not numerous today (perhaps they never have been) and their witness is not enough. Few are those who can search out and make contact with them. Again, there is the testimony of ordinary individuals in society who have themselves found human fulfillment through their inherited or adopted religious tradition. Such persons, however, can usually be of help only to others of like persuasion. Finally, the numerous prayer groups and other movements—Christian and non-Christian—that have recently sprung up in the West provide similar testimony. Though they are an inspiration to many, there are great numbers of people whom their witness cannot reach.

The vast majority of men and women have not yet realized their full potentiality as humans through their inherited or adopted religion. Such spiritually undernourished persons need something more readily available than the witness of gurus or inspiring individuals or groups. For them a renewal of personal allegiance to the sun can perform this function effectively. Recovery of attentiveness to the sun and to its spiritual meaning, as I myself have found, deepens our recognition of its meaning for us. Better still, it becomes a door to reverent and affectionate relationship with all the living organisms and all the inorganic matter we encounter in our daily life on earth, and finally—at least potentially—with life and matter elsewhere.

Those who are, knowingly or unknowingly, undernourished spiritually by their own religious traditions would not be the only ones to benefit from such a renewal. As I have noted earlier, there are others, and not the least of all in Christian lands, who though serious minded cannot accept the age-old contentions of established religion. They feel no need to believe in a personal supernatural reality as the source of (as they see it) a self-existing universe of continuously evolving or at least continuously changing matter and energy. For them the sun should be a logical focus for attention and provide a fertile source of respectful, even wondering, appreciation.

To be gifted with gratitude for what we owe to our environment, and with wonder at our situation in the cosmos, is surely its own reward. Sufficient reason for wonder lies, surely, in the sun's possibly fortuitous but none the less fortunate emergence from a cloud of hydrogen and helium in the locality that was to be, simply because of its emergence, *our* locality. Equal reason for gratitude, in the fact that just the right amount of matter other than hydrogen and helium was present, disposed in just the right way, to allow for the developing not only of life but of what we call self-awareness. The more we think about these matters, the more the wonder and gratitude will grow; the less we shall take them for granted. More important, in learning to be gratefully and wonderingly aware of the sun's central place in our material environment, those of us who have paid it scant attention can be learning to respond to it as fully as we have it in us to respond. In doing so we may learn to treasure, in its nowness, the total objective world that the sun makes possible. And, of course, whatever portion of it at any particular moment makes up our own immediate universe.

In the East, Buddhists speak of cherishing a feeling of gratitude even though there is actually, they say, neither personal self to be grateful nor personal God to be grateful to. For those who neither conceive of nor worship a personal God, it may be appropriate to express their gratitude daily in some such way. Such an expression of gratitude, whether by a believer or an unbeliever, is an excellent way to begin paying off one's debt to the physical environment.

* * *

The sun is peculiarly apt as a symbol of the world around us because it is actually far more than a symbol. In one sense it *is* our environment. We can never sufficiently impress on our minds what it means for us as living beings—and as thinking human beings. When we observe the sun, we are looking at what happens when the naked energy within the atom is unleashed. As the ancient peoples no doubt sensed more or less clearly, without this spring of energy none of the objects—living or nonliving—in our world could have come into being or could continue as they are. When we look at the sun we are looking not only at an uninterrupted hydrogen explosion: we are looking at the development of the solar system and at our own past evolution as a species, and at our potentiality for the future as well. The whole extent of our immediate physical surroundings, every aspect of our objective world in its nowness, depends in one way or another on the sun and its near presence. As we have noted, our earth-life system owes to this living star, this delicately balanced orb of furiously burning gases, not only its incredibly protracted development. It owes to it, too, the present and continuing existence of everything that lives and moves and reproduces within it.

The molecular structures in earth's core and mantle and surface soil, the emergence of life-giving water, the presence of life-sustaining atmosphere, owe their existence to it. The sensitivity in microorganisms and plants, the marvelous adaptations for speed and propagation in fishes and other aquatic life, the precise organization in the bodies of insects (even the smallest of them) and in some of their societies, the uncanny alertness in reptiles and in birds, the impressive degree of consciousness in mammals on land or in the sea, and finally the phenomenon of mutation and the process of natural selection implicit in the evolution of the myriad species of living creatures—all these factors could manifest themselves out of a primal material chaos only because of the sun's perfectly positioned presence. And no less the imperceptibly gradual development of the cellular structure of the human body, the infinitely complex nervous system, the incredibly elaborate organs of perception, the emergence of thought and finally of self-awareness in human beings—with their capacity for selfless and self-serving emotion and reasoning and decision, for probing the organization of the atom and the far reaches of the visible universe, and for arriving at logical conclusions and compelling moral judgments.

In a way, our very want of attention to the sun may be seen as a tribute to its all-importance for us. The fact of our taking it for granted might appear to indicate better than any words its ultimacy and, indeed, immediacy for us. Who, after all, thinks of the beating of the heart? Still, this sort of off-hand tribute to the sun seems more appropriate for the other creatures in nature than for humans. Simply because of their comparative lack of self-awareness, other living creatures are continuously helping to preserve the balance of nature. Theirs is a mute witness to the sun's all-importance for them. We humans cannot afford, however, to take the sun for granted any longer. Aware of the delicate balance that has preserved nature's continuing processes up to recent times, we have nevertheless begun, to our own and everything else's peril, to interfere with them. Through recognizing our debt to the sun, we should inevitably come to recognize more fully our responsibility to the physical environment it has brought into being.

Here, surely, lies an antidote for the loss of a sense of community with nature that is so much deplored today. Perhaps the situation is not as desperate or as widespread as is sometimes believed. But to whatever extent it does exist, our alienation from nature stems in large part from our alienation from the sun. To turn our attention back to it would be, for ordinary men and women, to restore and redeem our failing spirituality and so our sense of belonging to the world of nature and the fellowship of humankind. Here, too, we could look for one very practical result. The current and very proper stress on ecology by an informed few would then be inspired by a deeper sense of joyous participation. Efforts in the direction of conservation would become less aggressive, more spontaneous, than they sometimes now appear, accompanied as they so often are by righteous indignation against those who "exploit" nature without regard for the natural world or the future of humanity. Being unforced, they might no longer stir violent antagonisms and misunderstandings, but rather persuade others of the practical value of sharing in nature's grand design without competing with it.

* * *

We arrive now at a practical question: How we are to come to terms with the sun in everyday life and what we can expect personally from the relationship?

First of all, how are we to think with any accuracy about it? Just as there is no place from which the universe can be seen precisely *as* it is, so there is no place on earth from which we can see the sun precisely *where* it is. Turning as we do at a speed of more than one thousand miles an hour on our own axis, we perceive the sun to be moving. Actually, it is we who move, while the sun (though, like earth, turning on its own axis) stands still in relation to us—both sun and earth, of course, pursuing their immense orbit about the center of the galaxy. And depending on our position in our own 365¼-day orbit around the sun, we in the Northern Hemisphere perceive it to be traveling nearer and nearer to the southern horizon or farther and farther from it. All this may seem painfully obvious, but it is obvious only theoretically, not as a matter of personal experience. It would seem that we are condemned never to relate to the sun correctly so far as its position (and our own) is concerned.

Fortunately there is one qualified exception to the statement that we cannot see the sun precisely where it is. At midday, in most parts of the earth, we can observe our situation in relation to the sun more or less as it is. At this time the sun is "right here" above us, and we are "right here" below it. At other times, because the sun does not move in relation to ourselves, it continues (from its own standpoint) to be "right here," and we who slant away from it or slant toward it as the earth turns are somewhere "out there."

Airplane pilots, who know the experience of an outside loop, or astronauts, who know the sensations of weightlessness and freedom from a sense of up and down, can perhaps come nearest to picturing our situation realistically. As for the rest of us, instinct tells us we cannot afford to interfere with the "convenient lies" of earth life. And so we refuse—at least very many of us do—to think and see consistently in terms of our true situation. Habitually we think (no matter what we may say) of our heads as "up," though in the context of the solar system (and not of an earth pictured as independent of the celestial bodies around it) they are, except at midday, pointing out or down from the sun's "here."

Even so, it is quite possible through habitual correct thinking to learn gradually to picture the sun as standing still in relation to the earth and the earth not only as turning on its axis and orbiting around the sun, but as actually hanging in space as it rotates and orbits—and all this as taking place near the outer edge of a galaxy, the Milky Way, that is as far across as light can travel in 120,000 years—one of a seemingly innumerable host of such galaxies.

To achieve this sort of perception is not easy. When the idea first came home to me some years ago and my mind was still unused to such thinking, I once literally made myself dizzy by trying for most of a day to think of the earth and myself as turning toward and then away from the sun. Nor is this a state of mind one should remain immersed in continuously. Yet once we learn how to relate to the sun in space in this way, it is far easier to establish a fruitful personal relationship with it. And this we can manage by so training the mind that whenever it is idle—not concentrated on some legitimate concern of daily life in the outer or inner environment—it will automatically return to an attentiveness to the sun aloft in its stillness.

This sort of capacity is not merely a means of stepping off into a wider world. True, the sight of the sun dazzlingly present overhead can be a source of mental and spiritual refreshment. It can give us a remarkable sense of our own nowness and hereness. It can give us a sense of belonging to the universe. And in offering a vision of the immediate presence of cosmic power, it can foster an intense awareness of how much we depend on the ceaseless flow of that power. But it can also add an aesthetic dimension to life. For anyone with the slightest poetic imagination, the sun, just as we see it—and as the ancients saw it—can be in itself a poem: a song of joyous affirmation on the part of one small region of the cosmos to the creative energy that works this wheeling universe. Whether as revealed in the mysterious promise of the dawn or in the grandiose fulfillment of sundown, in the splendor of its silence in a cloudless midday sky or in the majesty of its stillness as seen through traveling clouds, it is for humans a celebration of being and life. It shines as the naked face of physical reality.

The sun as it may be repeatedly and directly experienced by us each day, now and here, can be infinitely more affecting to those with a little imagination than the sun we have all learned about in school or with the intellect. For such persons it can be in a very real sense the "golden disk" that the Hindu sage tells us of, which covers the door of Truth.

WHERE YOU BLAZE

Tireless you wait.
We turn from you, still Sun,
each hour, each mote of time,
tracking our purposes
as if you were not there.
Through the sheer midday sky
you cast your potent rays,
Nourisher, Guide,
reach down your lively hands,
uphold us, every one.
Yet we look anywhere
but where you blaze
and are.

And when your face is veiled,
such clouds as come
swallow all memory
but of themselves, till we
partake the stuff of them.
Tireless you wait,
sensing that one sure day
we shall turn back to you,
still Sun:
knowing that you are he
without whom we should not
have brains enough
even to forget.

* * *

Among the early results of a conscious openness to the sun, if one lives in the country, is a new attentiveness to and grateful appreciation of elemental matter: the earth, rock, sand, water, air, fire—and their combinations—that provide the substance of organic shapes and their means of nourishment and shelter. At-homeness with the sun spells increasing at-homeness with these, too. Behind all the indispensable component parts of our physical environment, and behind the various displays of the weather

—sunshine, clouds, rain, thunderstorms, hurricanes, earth-quakes, droughts—stretch vistas of interrelatedness for the watchful mind to explore.

If one lives in a city, the results of such thinking, though finally the same, are not so easily come by. Hence occasional visits to the mountains or the plains or the seaside are helpful as a spur to finding at-homeness with the physical environment—visits to any place where the pressing immediate concerns of everyday life cannot distract us from the business of learning to be attentive to it.

Most heartwarming of all, to open oneself to the sun is to win a far closer intimacy with sentient life on earth and thus an intuitive understanding of the interrelatedness of living beings of every kind. I can personally attest to feeling far closer to the creatures of nature (and to human beings, too) since recognizing my relationship to the sun and trying to intensify my awareness of it.

At the country place where I began writing this book there was not only a plentiful supply of songbirds and chipmunks; rabbits, groundhogs, and foxes; lizards and moles and snakes; wild ducks, wild geese, deer, and so on. There was also a host of domesticated animals. With them, thanks to intimacy with the sun, I developed a more than usual affinity—unmixed, I hope, with any lingering sense of human "superiority." With several of the farm animals, and notably a fourteen-year-old donkey, a special relationship sprang up: there seemed on occasion to be something like a transfer of thought.

There were also, naturally, innumerable spiders, grasshoppers, beetles, ants, grubs, worms, deerflies, crickets, and other insects large and small—including occasionally a startling praying mantis with swiveling, pointed head and great bug eyes. Opportunities were plentiful to stop and marvel at their fascinating and intricate structures. But I came to look upon them, too, with respect and something like love, and to treat them accordingly.

Sometimes I have been privileged to enter just a bit into the hidden life of small creatures I could never have expected to know intimately. In a moss garden I made in a glass bowl, I placed a small charcoal-black newt that I happened to turn up under a stone as I was collecting lichens in the woods near my cottage. Before I released it, it lived for a number of days on a diet of armadillolike sowbugs and other small insects that I managed (hardheartedly) to supply it with. One day I happened to be watching it just as it had started to shed its skin. It skillfully helped the circular roll to move backwards down its body by shrugging its tiny shoulders, and after squirming about a bit, finally managed to persuade it over its hips. When the newt emerged, shiny and fresh, it doubled back on itself and snapped up the cast-off skin as if it were a fly.

Several years before this writing, I was privileged to observe the growth from eggs to maturity of some larvae of the cecropia moth. After their hatching I kept the larvae in a large carton covered with nylon netting and supplied them with fresh wild cherry leaves (the only leaves they would eat) for about two months. At first they were very small, spiny black things. As they devoured the tender leaves, they quickly passed through a dusky yellow stage (still with black spines) and then three green ones. Each time they shed their skins, they took on a new appearance: with their bright red and blue and yellow (and finally also orange) knobs, or "tubercules," they were objects of fascinating beauty to rival a master jeweler's work.

At last one day I noticed the largest of the larvae, by this time perhaps three inches long, moving restlessly about the carton under the nylon netting. Sensing that it was ready to weave a cocoon, I placed leaves and twigs where I thought they might be useful. To my gratification, I found after a time that it had begun painstakingly making its house for the winter among them. The head was tirelessly moving back and forth, attaching the silk that flowed in its mouth, now here, now there. Gradually the covering, at first sheer and gauzelike, became more and more opaque. All I could see now was a hint of the head's untiring motion. Then it was completely hidden by the fabric it was weaving, which by now was turning from cream white to light brown.

How long it must have kept on working inside I realized the following spring when, after I had removed the cocoon from the refrigerator where it had been stored, the enchanting rose and gray and white and pale tan moth emerged. Under the tough outer layer of the cocoon that I had seen the larva weave, I found a porous section, no doubt to protect the delicate pupa from shocks, and inside that another impervious layer like the outside one. In it was the shriveled skin of the once fat green worm. It was an unforgettable experience to have observed the life cycle of this beautiful, gracefully proportioned large moth through each of its bodily stages.

It is possible, also, to establish some sort of relationship with plants. Having a flower garden has been almost a necessity since my parents first encouraged my brothers and me to have our private ones in childhood. Recently I have returned to an enthusiasm that I indulged for a number of years as an adolescent: the hybridizing of irises. Now, many years later, I am becoming familiar with a bit of genetics and experimenting with the fabulous new varieties—especially reblooming irises—that are being introduced each year. It is a unique pleasure to watch the blooming of an iris plant one has brought indoors in late fall.

REBLOOMING IRIS

I love you—so fresh and still, so
welcome here in my south-looking
study window this twelfth day of December.
It isn't fair, perhaps, to be able to
take you out of my garden and
have you bloom, yellow and fragrant and
glistening in mid-morning sun,
when you put up your flower stem a whole
month too late and should have been
wasted by the timely frosts that
seized the rest of your kind just a
few days after I brought you indoors
in your comfortable pot.
No doubt if you deserved to survive
you would have tried reblooming
a month or so earlier. But just now
the very fact of your blooming at all—

so gracious, so floating—in this
small warm room, with that vague hint of
wintergreen in your fragrance,
allows me to make of you my
total universe for this one moment.
That surely justifies whatever
indiscretion I was guilty of in
defying the order of nature—doesn't it?
And by all that is fair ought to
excuse your indiscretion too.

I realize today that my experiments of sixty years ago were most unscientifically carried out. Even then, though, I was captivated by the graceful and balanced structure of the flower, its cool fragrance, and the remarkable means it had developed during the millennia of its evolution for cross-pollenation. The positioning of the anther with its male pollen just where a bumblebee can brush it off with his hairy back as he pushes his way down under the style arm to get honey, and then rub it onto the female stigma flap at the tip of the next style arm as he passes under, has always seemed to me one of nature's neatest developments for ensuring the evolution of a genus. While the rootstocks, or "rhizomes," provide for the perpetuation of the individual variety, the seeds ensure change and often progress: flowers of iris seedlings, unlike those of annual plants, many times differ from those of the parent plants.

I cannot be sure that there is a direct relation between one's feelings for plants and their growth, as some people maintain. Many of them grow profusely for me without my giving them any attention. Some hardly grow no matter how carefully I tend and encourage them. Perhaps in many such relationships with plants, where a person feels some sort of response, what happens is that the mind is given a chance to listen to *itself*. Yet frequently on a hot summer day, watering wild ferns transplanted from the woods to a rock garden, I have acutely sensed how much they (or was it I?) relished the sprinkling I was giving their plumelike fronds.

Like others who live in the country, I have had pleasant and instructive experiences with wild birds. Especially while watching them as they have come in droves to feed on the sunflower and other seed I spread for them in winter and spring. I was struck by the fact that in very harsh winter weather even the most forward of the larger birds, such as bluejays, would from time to time retire to a nearby tree and give others a chance to feed. Once, when I put out seed for a whole summer, I watched a pair of cardinals bring three broods of young in succession (two each time). They actually chased away the more mature offspring of the same season when they came to feed with the younger, less experienced ones.

Certainly my most endearing experience of intimacy with a bird came one day at the retreat in the Thousand Islands where I went each summer with Swami Nikhilananda from 1948 to 1962.

A MIDDAY BATH

In blinding heat one summer day
Wood ferns breathed in gratefully
The hose-fed shower I lightly played
Over their listless, shadowed bed,
Where the transplanted elegance
Of once benignly spreading fronds
Wilted like weary angels' wings,
When, somewhere near the prominence
Of rock I stood on—quick, intense,
Importunate, and unannounced—
I sensed a rash intruder there.
A thrilling presence in the air
Like an arrested meteor,
An iridescent flash of green
Borne upon wings that worked unseen
In a gray cloud of mist behind,
Told me, as recognition stirred,
My hose had lured a hummingbird.

Skirting the edges of the spray
To test its truth, inquisitively
Venturing toward the enticing shower,
He hovered, hesitating still,
As if perplexed to reconcile
Need with mistrust. No tawny flower
Of tiger lily or trumpet vine
Drew the small shape of swiftness there,
But thirst and torrid heat combined
Tempted his unaccustomed mind
To try indifference to fear.

Now, for my unbelieving eyes,
Inventive dooms and destinies
Worked up a comedy more rare
Than any playwright, anywhere,
Could have concocted from his brain's
Widest-eyed imaginings;
For as I waited, still entranced,
The magic creature, for this once
Sporting in unfeigned innocence,
Settled on a convenient stone
And sat there, clothed in nonchalance,
Squirming delectable surprise
To share the water's clarities.
Shaking his lightly opened wings,
Preening his feathers into place,
Turning his head from side to side
Precautiously, though unafraid,
He bathed at his contented ease—

While my hose, its task long done,
Centered on this droll play alone,
Until, the glad ablutions ended,
Quit of the calm his need commanded,
Without a single glance at me
He suddenly rose and streaked away.

Many people enjoy something of this sort of intimacy with creatures of nature, no doubt, without having first become consciously intimate with the sun. This was true in my own case. But an already developed sensitivity to living creatures and a growing desire to do injury to as few of them as possible have undoubtedly been heightened by my recent attentiveness to the sun. There is no reason why this should not prove true for others, as well.

At-homeness with the sun reveals a further dimension in our relation to individual creatures of nature. It is an intuitive awareness of them as integral parts of the whole environment. I know of it because of experiencing certain states where poetic intuition of the sun's meaning for all living beings takes over. Such states involve an intense momentary identification of oneself with the whole of the outer environment that one is in contact with, and an identification of each perceived object in that world with the whole. It is impossible to convey in words more than a faint echo of the actual experience. Only when someone has made a sustained effort to know the sun, and enjoyed the results, will he or she fully read between the lines of any description.

A VISIT

> Quick, clear-eye, curve-bill
> Carolina wren,
> Perched inquisitive, cautious,
> Here on my windowsill—
> Warm brown above, buff white beneath,
> Your tail erect,
> Over your blinking eye
> A thin white feather line,
> Inside your round breast
> Short, measured heaves of breath
> Or (who's to say?) heartbeat—
>
> Out of your smallness flares,
> Explodes,
> The echoing miracle of a sun,

Of planets coalesced in space,
Arcs of unnumbered years
Slow-drawn through time,
Green algae and sea things,
Of cold-blood reptiles
Blinking-eyed as you,
Dim, tentative winged shapes,
On down to your hot-blood fragility.

You tilt your nervous head to eye
My giant window pane,
You stretch your neck
And lift to your full height,
And (though I hope you look for me)
Raptly peer, I guess,
At yourself mirrored there.
Bold-shy little one,
Tell me, before you slip away,
What does that brief yawn of yours
Convey?

All this, and far more, we can anticipate in establishing a personal relationship with the sun—begetter not only of physical matter but of organic life as we know it. As we increasingly turn our attention toward it, the details of the world of the sun that we encounter become increasingly real. We achieve a devoted attentiveness to all of them and our eyes are opened to further realms of insight—an insight that, as humans, is available to each of us.

* * *

In theory, to win through to anything like full awareness of our relationship to the sun and full attentiveness to any details of the world of the sun immediately confronting us, we have to achieve a constantly flowing sense of its presence. Something like what mystics would call a sense of the presence of God or ultimate reality. Such an experience, we are led to believe by authorities on spiritual discipline, comes to one only through an unflagging effort of will; it cannot endure without a daily practice continued over a long period of time. This sort of effort, they tell us, is best suited to those with uninterrupted hours for practice, such as, for instance, yogis or Zen or other contemplative monastics. Ordinary men and woman are in no position to exert the unflagging effort that such specially equipped persons exhibit. That is why it has usually been assumed that only those who retire from the world are capable of anything like sustained mystical experience.

My assumption here, based on my own intuitive experience (however modest), is quite different. Unflagging effort is indeed required, but if there is a sustained bent of mind toward the desired goal, the effort need not be heroically strenuous. Those who sincerely desire the sort of awareness we are talking about here will cherish a consistent dissatisfaction with their present state of understanding, which, as they realize, deprives them of their right to know things as they are. But they will adopt a more relaxed approach, one that makes use of such limited means as their special circumstances allow. It is not necessary that that dissatisfaction remain always on the conscious level, so long as it always returns when everyday distractions no longer interfere.

Ordinary men and women will have to be content with a gradually intensified awareness of the sun's life-giving presence and of the infinitely varied world it sustains. Yet as they follow this more relaxed approach, they may confidently expect that the awareness they finally obtain will not fade, but, like the sun itself, will continue unfailingly to enlighten and sustain them. It is cultivating this more relaxed approach that has been our chief business in this first stage of our journey on the Road to Now—the only approach available to most of us for becoming truly at home with our immediate physical environment. Without an awareness of what we owe to the sun, we cannot begin to fathom the depth— and the breadth—of the second aspect of our environment, the psychological world within us.

✵ THE NOW OF THE SELF

RECOGNITION

Looking in each face,
You sense through every one
A presence, fathomless
As an unclouded sun,

That, from while to while,
Looks back in your eye
To come at and assess
Your own deep instancy.

So far as I can remember, until I entered college I had scarcely
a thought about the inner world of the self. I had lived a
joyously pagan life, almost completely immersed in the world of
the senses. During the four years of college I began to be aware
of states of mind involving youthful emotions and imaginings of
various sorts. Yet I probably never stood back to observe them
dispassionately, but identified myself with them uncritically. No
doubt because of philosophy courses I took in those years (one
was a survey of Western philosophy and another, as I recall, dealt
with the philosophy of religion), I began thinking soon after
graduation about "the Absolute" and conceived it as something
that could be attained through mental discipline. I even wrote
quite a long, and no doubt highly theoretical, treatise (now lost)
on the subject. About this time, readings—first in Buddhism and
then in Hindu religious thought—intensified my interest in the
world of the self. As things turned out, it was to Hinduism that
I finally gave my full attention.

The first works on Hinduism that I read were collections of

lectures by the prophetlike Vivekananda, delivered in America in the 1890s. They dealt with the four basic disciplines, or "yogas," for attaining union with Brahman, or ultimate reality—what I had once vaguely thought of as the Absolute. These four disciplines, related to intellect, emotion, mental concentration, and activity, are the ways of intuitive wisdom, devotional self-giving, conscious mental control, and service in the spirit of human community. The one that was spiritually the most "practical" (and also esoteric) and therefore claimed most of my attention at first was the way of conscious mental control.

Vivekananda's *Raja-Yoga* is the book that deals with this subject and that, incidentally, has been a source of much of the information used later by popular writers on mental yoga in the West. From it I learned for the first time the Hindu diagram of the mind, or "inner organ" as it is called. It embraces the mind-stuff (*chitta*), which is normally full of waves (desire, aversion, and so on) but which this yoga proposes to control, and the various mental functions, such as memory (*manas*), ego (*ahamkara*), and discriminative intellect (*buddhi*). In addition to discussing the elements of Hindu psychology, the book outlines exercises for controlling and concentrating the mind.

After reading this work, I began practicing some of the exercises each morning after arising and each night before going to sleep. And this despite the explicit warning by Vivekananda that with few exceptions they should be taken up *only* under the guidance of a qualified teacher. (I, of course, felt I was one of the exceptions!) What claimed my attention most at the time was its exercises for controlling the breathing. Some of them were prescribed to calm the mind in preparation for meditation. These involved simply rhythmic breathing or slightly regulated breathing (as, for instance, inhaling while counting four, holding the breath while counting sixteen, exhaling while counting eight). But other exercises prescribed were more difficult: retaining the breath in the lungs or excluding the breath from them for extended periods. Instead of confining myself to the simpler exercises as aids to mental quiet, I took up the others and made them an end in themselves. Gradually I carried them to extreme lengths.

The fascination they held was something like what I had felt earlier in looking directly at the sun. When I practiced the breathing exercises my eyes were shut, and so I naturally focused on the state of my mind. Here, too, I was observing a reality more central than the surface light of the mind. For as I became more and more proficient in holding the breath in or out, and no longer was forced to yield at once to the urge to gasp for air, a new experience dawned. The mind would be invaded, then literally carried away, by a flow of unmixed bliss—the way, in a partly cloudy sky, the air is at first slowly brightened as the sun reaches the edge of a cloud that has been hiding it, and then is flooded with clear light. It was much like the access of bliss one sometimes feels, briefly, on hearing certain passages of music, but even more pure and protracted. So intoxicating was this bliss that I had not the slightest wish to return from it. Whenever it came, which was not infrequently, there was no longer any sense of needing to breathe—only the persuasive authority of the blissful state. I cannot recall how much time was required to arouse it, but it took at least a minute, I think. And until the bliss began to flow, I usually had to exercise will power so as not to revert to the normal rhythm of breathing.

I then mistakenly believed that I was nearing the goal of the spiritual quest. It would be a long time before I heard that a "spiritual experience" has to result in a definite loss or at least diminishing of ego-centeredness if it is to be regarded as a valid experience. Nevertheless, no matter how intense the feeling, some urge of common sense always made me will to start breathing again before I lost consciousness. Possibly the urge manifested itself only when I began thinking about the bliss instead of remaining merged in its flow. Besides, one fact warned me that something was amiss. After I had been practicing the exercises for a number of days, I began to find that at night, on completing them, the normal automatic action of the lungs did not reassert itself unless I consciously breathed in and out for a time. Finally I gave up the practice, and after a short while it was again difficult to hold the breath in or out for longer than about twenty seconds.

Later I read somewhere that a sense of bliss is manifested in the mind when a person is drowning, as the carbon dioxide in the blood rises above a certain level. If what I read is accurate, this would also be the case, obviously, when no oxygen is supplied to the blood during the exercises of retaining or excluding the breath. But I doubt that the bliss can be dismissed as being simply the result of this one physical cause. As I said, what I experienced was, though more pure and protracted, a bliss of the same order as that which an aesthetically sensitive person can experience through inspired music or other works of art while breathing normally. Hence retaining or excluding the breath for long periods, with its raising of the blood's carbon dioxide content, may be seen as one of several means to trigger—though not cause—the experience of bliss.

An even more arresting experience of the inner world took place several years later, when I was about twenty-four years old. I was studying musical composition and living in the country. By now I was somewhat familiar with Hindu religious thought, though for several years previously I had given my attention mostly to music. At the time I speak of, a reawakened interest had caused me to begin rereading Vivekananda's lectures. I also read for the first time Romain Rolland's *Life of Ramakrishna,* the remarkable story of the life of Vivekananda's saintly master. I had not yet been formally initiated by a spiritual teacher, or guru, and would first make personal contact with Swami Nikhilananda, with whom I was to work for more than twenty-five years and was already corresponding, later in this same year of 1932. But every day, in my free time, I went to a nearby woods and, sitting on a tree stump, practiced a sort of meditation. This meant for me the repeating of certain inspiring passages from Hindu scripture or mystical writings along with an attempt to grasp their meaning.

One day, instead of going into the woods, I sat in a straight chair in my room and began practicing a mental exercise described in Vivekananda's *Raja-Yoga* for use with one of the simpler exercises in breathing. I tried to picture two nerve currents supposed by yogis to pass along the spinal column on the left and right. As I drew in the breath and briefly retained it, I imagined a current passing down the left side and forcefully striking the plexus, or, as yogis call it, "lotus," at the base of the spine. Whether as a result of some physiological effect or a subtle mental stimulation, I at once became aware that my body was a mass of vibrations. After a time I opened my eyes, which until then had remained shut. So intense was the sense of vibrations that I found my body to be nothing but that mass of highly charged movement —not luminous, yet very clearly some sort of vibration, and not flesh and blood and bone. Gradually the impression faded out. Though on several occasions I tried to reproduce the experience by repeating the preliminaries, I never succeeded. This, perhaps more than anything that I had experienced previously, convinced me that I was progressing spiritually.

I must add here that when I first met Swami Nikhilananda face to face and told him of my experiences, he said at once, "Knock that sort of thing out of your head." To this day I am grateful for that brusque but friendly order. It warned me that to allow oneself to take insignificant psychic happenings seriously is to miss the chief aim of spiritual life: attenuation of the sense of separate, autonomous ego and of preoccupation with its concerns. It is hardly different from taking the fascinating pseudomystical experiences a person may have under nitrous oxide gas (I myself have had them on a few occasions) as holding deep spiritual meaning, or from imagining that the "mind-expanding" effects of marijuana, heroin, cocaine, or the hallucinogens are the real thing, mystically speaking.

In referring to attenuation of ego, I do not mean to disparage the importance of a healthy ego-self for normal everyday living. Obviously, for most of us life cannot go on without the cooperation of a disciplined ego. Nor do I mean to imply, in referring to the various drugs, that they may not in some instances reveal to users the existence of deeper layers of the mind.

At the time of my meeting with the swami, his remark taught me where *not* to look if I was interested in something more than phenomena—namely, the basics of spiritual life. Still, the phenomena themselves had revealed to me areas of the mind whose existence I had not previously proved through personal experience.

* * *

It was after encountering Hindu thought that I first came to pay serious attention to the second aspect of our environment, the self and its world. As mentioned in the prologue, to deal meaningfully with the self requires caution. Any intuition or concept about it can be self-defeating. Our best approach will be to familiarize ourselves first with the world of the self seen as soul or person. Here we can be objective without danger of grossly misrepresenting the subject of our inquiry.

Acquaintance with the Hindu religious philosophy of Advaita, or strict Nondualism, helped me form my first clear conception of the individual soul. Exponents of this school of thought see reality as an indivisible or nondual whole—hence its designation as Nondualism. Their basic conception of the soul grew out of profound mystical experiences reported by certain Vedic sages in early times, and set forth in treatises composed perhaps a thousand years after the scripture in which occurs the invocation to the sun quoted in the first chapter. These sages claimed that in their meditations they had come face-to-face with, achieved communion with, an indivisible, eternal, all-knowing, all-joyous reality—a reality undergirding and giving identity to the individual human soul. This reality they named Atman (it is what Ralph Waldo Emerson aptly called the Oversoul).

The doctrines of Advaita have been termed the "theology of identity." Thinkers of this school contend, on the basis of scriptural statements and of their own mystical experience, that there is actually no difference between the individual human soul and this Oversoul; it is this Oversoul that enlightens and gives life to the human person. Not only all humans but all sentient beings partake of it. It is indispensable to the existence of each and every one of them.

In everyday life, however, none of us is aware of our essential identity with Atman or the Oversoul. The soul that all of us are aware of sees itself as separate from the rest of reality and very often assumes itself to be not only real in itself but self-sufficient and gifted with free will. Thinkers of the Advaita school hold that the soul's separate reality and feeling of independent self-sufficiency are only apparent, not ultimately real. The individual soul, they say, is the Oversoul overcome, as it were, by an ignorance or forgetfulness of its true nature. Because they see this limited soul as the principle of individual awareness, they sometimes describe it as a spark or a reflection of the Oversoul.

The term these thinkers use to denote the individual soul is *jiva*, which literally means "living being." It is the soul that all of us who have not achieved mystical insight identify ourselves with in everyday life. Thinkers of this school maintain that during its state of forgetfulness, while it looks on itself as an independent being, it is to all intents and purposes real. According to them, this limited soul is born, dies, and is reborn in a fresh body as a result of its desires and actions in past lives, for the purpose of gathering further experience. Finally, when it has learned through repeated experience that desire is never satisfied by the fulfilling of desire, it turns away from egoistic exploitation of the world of the senses and in the end rediscovers its true nature. The doctrine of the soul's repeated rebirth (not necessarily always in an upward direction) is known as the theory of reincarnation.

In one of the principal Hindu scriptures the individual soul is described as being encased in five "sheaths." These are the sheaths of food (that is, flesh), of nervous energy, of memory, of discriminative intellect, and of joy. They represent the different powers of the soul and the different areas of experience available to it. They are said to be successively interior to one another, the sheath of joy being the innermost and "nearest" to the soul. And the soul is spoken of as being encased in them all. To look on these sheaths as being literally within one another, however, is not quite what is intended. The meaning here is, according to a leading ninth-century religious philosopher of the Advaita or strict Nondualistic school, that each successive sheath is subtler than the one "outside" it and actually pervades it. The light of the individual soul, also called Atman as spark of the Oversoul, is said to permeate all the sheaths. At the same time, as Oversoul it remains in reality unattached to them.

Most of the time the individual soul mistakenly identifies itself with one or another of the sheaths. Generally it experiences them (and identifies itself with them) in varying combinations. At times it may experience one of them almost exclusively—as, for instance, when it is absorbed in observing a sunset or in enjoying a fragrant flower or a carefully prepared meal, in listening to inspired music, in sexual pleasure, in the excitement of hope or fear, in recollection of things past, in the exercise of reason, in aesthetic or spiritual rapture. I have sometimes wondered if my own experience of my body as a mass of vibrations might not—if this Hindu analysis is a valid one—have been a brief glimpse of the sheath of nervous energy. And whether my experiences of intense bliss during the retention or exclusion of the breath might not have been connected with the sheath of joy.

The separate individual soul as conceived by followers of the Advaita theology of identity corresponds to the immortal soul spoken of in the devotional sects of Hinduism. These hold the soul to be either intimately related to a personal God or eternally distinct from and dependent on God, and to be permanently real instead of, in the Advaita view, apparently real. As already noted, it is this phenomenal soul that is born, feels desires and performs actions to fulfill them, dies, and (after possibly going to a temporary heaven or hell) is reborn on earth according to its past desires and actions, for further experience leading to eventual union with God.

Followers of the nondevotional Advaita school, believing the individual soul to be essentially one with the ever free Oversoul, hold that whatever sense of free will it enjoys derives from its true relation to the Oversoul. The very mechanism of rebirth—what is known as the "law of karma"—is based on the assumption that men and women possess freedom of choice to carry out or not to carry out an action. Both devotional and nondevotional Hindus teach, though for different reasons, that actions performed without egoistic attachment to their results have no power to impede the soul's onward progress.

For Hindus of all persuasions the individual soul we have been talking about is not indissolubly joined to the physical body but is distinct from it. The soul is associated with the body only during its present life, but it retains its association with all the sheaths except the sheath of flesh in its successive lives until it realizes its true relation to God, or the Oversoul. In achieving this realization it attains the goal of human life: knowledge of who it really is.

* * *

To prepare ourselves for coming to know how we as individu-

als directly experience the world of the self, we may also take a
brief look at some Christian ideas about the soul. So far as I am
aware, the Christian scriptures, unlike the scriptures of the Hindus, never spell out in anything like precise terms what they mean
by the word *soul.* That became the task of the early theologians
known as Church Fathers. The Old Testament, however, provides a profound insight into the soul when it states that God, in
creating human beings, said, "Let us make man in our image,
after our likeness."

In Christian belief God is ultimate being, and all God's creatures possess being. But human resemblance to God lies in the
soul. God possesses personality, God is spirit. Men and women,
through their souls, are persons, and their souls are spiritual. It
must be understood that what we call personality, as humans
know it, is really an inexpressible mystery—as indefinable as it is
immediate. So too, God, who is ultimate mystery, is beyond expression in words or objective thought. But what is meant by
personality in God can be most nearly grasped by intuitive
thought in terms of what it seems to mean in ourselves. God is
also wisdom and power, and above all, love. The human person
thinks and knows, wills, and loves.

The soul is the life in humans. This life is the source of their
activity, growth and development, and sensation. But human
beings, say Christians, also possess a spiritual principle of life
which, unlike the principle of life in plants and animals, is the
source of their intelligence and freedom of choice. Created by
God out of nothing, the soul enjoys immortality in heaven after
death—according to some Christians, usually following a period
of purgation—or endures it in hell, where it remains eternally
deprived of conscious awareness of God's presence. Its destiny,
as all but those of Calvinist persuasion believe, is determined
through God's grace and its own free choice.

Here lies the inner meaning of the story of Adam and Eve, who
stand for the soul in man and woman. Humans, say Christian
thinkers, though made in the image and likeness of God, chose
to be like God *in their own way* rather than in God's way, whereby
they would have remained united to God in love and so shared
in the divine nature. It was pride and disobedience—traits of

self-will—that caused Adam and Eve, and their descendants, to lose their intimate awareness of God's presence. In Christian belief it was God's sacrifice in Jesus Christ that opened the way for men and women to return, if they so willed, to God's way. The human soul, being made in God's image, is gifted with both intelligence and freedom of choice. God's sacrifice in Christ returned that gift, as it were, to humanity. The human soul was now free not only to turn away from God but to turn back again.

There is one notable difference between the Christian and Hindu views of the soul. For a Christian, a man or woman is one in body and soul: they constitute an undivided whole existing independently and not interchangeable with any other. Each is as much a part of the human being as the other: both the spiritual and the material part are real, and both are bound up with human destiny. The body is not something inferior or evil, not a prison for the soul, nor is it a mere tool of the soul. For the modern Roman Catholic Christian, the key word is now "person" rather than "soul."

For a Hindu the soul is not the physical body. The "sheath of flesh" is not bound up with the individual person's destiny except as a temporary means toward that person's progress toward God. At the same time, though in the Hindu view the soul discards the sheath of flesh at the moment of death, it remains identified with the other four: the sheaths of nervous energy, memory, discriminative intellect, and joy. Both views thus identify the soul with four fifths, as it were, of the human person—the Christians simply adding the extra fifth as sharing in its destiny. But the physical body disintegrates at death, and so, despite the emphasis in later times on a physical resurrection, it is doubtful that early Christians like Saint Paul thought of it in exactly these terms. When the soul rose from the grave to enjoy a life in the presence of God, they held, it would need a spiritual body, and it was this incorruptible body that the soul was identified with at the resurrection. It may turn out that the two doctrines are not as far apart as they appear. Both, moreover, make it clear that the soul's ultimate destiny is to have communion with God or ultimate reality.

* * *

The last word about the inner world of the person has not been said by any of the great religions. In the nineteenth century, psychologists and then psychoanalysts began research in this field that up to that time had been largely the province of theologians and mystics. Through their findings the concept of the inner world was vastly enlarged.

It was Sigmund Freud, of course, who first set out to systematically explore and analyze what had even before his time been called the subconscious or unconscious mind. Through analysis of patients' dreams he finally concluded that the human person's urges derive basically from what he called the libido, which is clearly but not uniquely manifested in the sex urge. As components of the person, he identified, in addition to the readily observable conscious mind, not only the layer called the dynamic unconscious, but also another called the preconscious. In his view, thoughts or urges held in the preconscious might easily be recalled, but those repressed in the unconscious could only be elicited through psychoanalytic techniques or by other techniques such as hypnosis. It was through his psychoanalytic research that the various stages of the sexual instinct's development—autoerotic, narcissistic, homosexual, and heterosexual—as well as the fact of their sublimation, became clearer. His research, like that of later psychoanalysts, was aimed not simply at gaining new scientific information but at helping patients achieve a healthier state of mind, allowing them to adjust more satisfactorily to the world around them. Freud later added to his diagram of the person such elements as the id (embodiment of the twin primal impulses to enjoyment and self-destruction), ego (where the reality principle reigns), and superego (related to conscience).

Sigmund Freud's explorations represent a true breakthrough. All later psychoanalysis is indebted to him. His basic findings and theories were the starting point from which Alfred Adler and Carl Jung, among others, developed their perhaps less dogmatic (but no less speculative) views. In place of the libido-oriented drive of the id, Adler isolated the goals of significance and power (related to the sense of inferiority) and a sense of community.

Carl Jung pushed the inquiry into the person farther by describing a number of types into which people may be separated. While some employ thought as a guide to judgment, he said, others employ feeling; while some experience their world and their relationships with others in terms of direct sense impressions, others do so more in terms of intuition. Thought, feeling, sense, and intuition are four "functions" of consciousness isolated by Jung, which he held to be responsible for the differentiation of types among humans. He spoke of the first two and the second two as related pairs of oppositions. One of the four functions, he said, takes a leading role in a person, and it is supported normally by only one from the other pair. Thus we may have an intellectual person who is intuitive in nature, or an emotional one who is sensual in nature, and so on. Jung saw the healthy person as making use of and balancing all four functions. Many of the difficulties people in the modern world encounter he attributed to disregard or suppression of the neglected functions.

It was Jung who elaborated the concepts of extravert and introvert. Extraversion he explained as the trend of the libido that involves an openness to the appeal of the object; introversion, as the trend that involves a concentration of interest in the subject. It was Jung's contention that a person should suppress or repress neither side of human nature, but be able to enjoy and direct all the basic capacities.

Jung spoke also of a faculty of the person by which one can release oneself from the sole claim of any member of the various possible pairs of opposed types. This he named the "transcendent function," which would thus be a fifth function of consciousness. This function, he said, works in us through the use of what we know as symbols and myths. By the method of "symbolization and mythologization," it releases names and things from what we associate them with in perceiving them or thinking about them. It thus helps us see them and their background as "delimited" picturings—to our faculties of thinking, feeling, sensing, and intuiting—of an "undelimited unknown," that is to say, of ultimate reality or God.

Our goal of complete alertness to the Now of things would appear to be related to Jung's concept of the healthy person. As we shall see, however, we aim to achieve it with as little objectification and intellectual analysis as possible.

Along with Adler, Jung recognized the significance of religious belief and experience for the human person. The individual's spiritual growth he explained in terms of a psychic energy that imbues every psychic level in accordance with the age and evolution of the individual. He also developed the concept of the collective unconscious, in which all human beings, and especially those of a particular culture, participate, and in which are located certain archetypes, or primordial potencies.

A few of Jung's remarks about the ego are relevant to our present discussion. In one of his works he points out what he calls "the important fact" in connection with consciousness: that there can be no such thing as consciousness unless there is an ego to which it refers. A relating of "psychic facts" to the ego is how he would define consciousness. As for ego itself, he describes it as, first, a general awareness of the body, and second, a long series of memories that attest to the fact of one's having existed in the past. This complex thing called ego, he says, attracts certain contents from the "dark realm" of the unconscious as well as impressions from the world outside. When any of these become associated with the ego they become conscious. As we shall see, the term *ego* as he uses it here is in some ways like our term *self*. But they are by no means identical, since the ego is equated by Jung with general awareness of the body and with memory. The ego, as we understand it, is essentially a function of thought. For us, the important thing about ego is that there can be no such thing as ego unless there is a self to which it refers.

A statement of Freud's about the unconscious also bears upon our discussion of the self. Freud explains how tentative our knowledge of it is. He draws a parallel with Immanuel Kant's conception of "phenomenon" and "noumenon," appearance and reality. The real nature of the unconscious, he observes, is just as inaccessible to consciousness as the "real" world (Kant's noumenal world behind the world we experience) is to our senses. It is every bit as imperfectly reported to us through what is given us by consciousness as the external world is reported to us through what the sense organs indicate of it. It should be noted that Freud's findings and theories, like Adler's and Jung's, deal with the structure of the inner world as a whole, with what Hindus would call the "inner organ" of the individual soul and Christians would call the person.

The pioneers in psychoanalysis have immensely increased our intellectual understanding of the total person. They have enlarged our vision of the subjective environment just as startlingly as astronomers and astrophysicists have enlarged our vision of the objective environment. The psychoanalytic view of the person, like the views of Hinduism and Christianity, is a realistic one and quite valid in its own frame of reference. But though the findings of psychologists and psychiatrists increase our familiarity with the overall design of the inner world, they contribute little more to our particular quest than do the earlier findings of theologians. Our purpose here, after acquainting ourselves with the individual soul, or person, or psyche, is to isolate the self.

If we take the whole, or even the greater part, of the inner environment to be the self, we cannot use it to become intimately at home with the details of that world as we meet with them. They remain confused in our thinking with the one observing them. We have no distinct entity to focus upon as symbol. And without a clear symbol, we cannot develop a spontaneous attentiveness to any of those details.

In a sense we *are* the soul, the person, the psyche. But the self, or true *I*, is, as it were, the soul of the soul, the person of the person, the psyche of the psyche. We must narrow our sights to find it. Despite the insights that all these researchers have yielded us, we are still left in the dark about *who* that central self is, *what* it is, and *where* it resides.

* * *

To average individuals, untrained in scientific method or philosophy or theology, it is quite obvious that one can and does actually know oneself in the immediate Now of the living moment. Such persons generally find it difficult if not impossible, however, to grasp the subtleties and niceties of the various psychological or theological distinctions about the soul or person or psyche, and to relate themselves to these distinctions. What they read about them exists, so far as they are concerned, in an intellectual realm quite outside their own immediate experience. All this may seem puzzling or even discouraging to them sometimes. Yet it hardly indicates that they or any of us ought to discipline our minds until we *can* grasp those subtle concepts. That we grasp an intellectual diagram of the self is not of great moment in our present enterprise.

The findings and diagrams of theologians and psychoanalysts are surely valuable in their own way and in their own place. But the self we are seeking to isolate here is the self intuitively known as "me" by each of us (not excluding the theologians and psychologists themselves). And our aim is not to learn what these speculative thinkers and researchers have decided that the human person is, but by attentiveness to the self to become ever more at home with *our own* inner environment in its immediate reality. So it is not enough to confine ourselves to others' findings and diagrams about the soul or person or psyche. We are driven back eventually to our own private encounter with the self, or true *I.* And here we become individually responsible for observations based on our own experience.

What then is *for us* this self we seek to be attentive to so as to become full-fledged human beings? How are we to identify it for ourselves, recognize it for what it is? And how, once we have found it, are we to relate to it personally, now and here?

We have to admit at once that though we feel we know the self and are in communion with it, what we habitually refer to as "me" is both closer to us and farther from us than the sun. To begin with, it appears to include, in experience, not just the whole mind but the whole body as thought of and sensed from within. Is this commonly held concept of one's self the entity we are looking for? The best answer to that question—for any fairly healthy-minded person concerned about the answer—is to be had by sitting down and experiencing the self at close range.

When I collect my thoughts to observe myself, seated in a straight chair and shutting my eyes to concentrate better, the first thing to claim attention as the mind clears is indeed (if I am alert) the shape of the body felt from within. It is the body, I feel, that encloses whatever I mean by "me." By the same token, however, it is *not* the self. Almost immediately I then become aware of the activity of breathing. "I am breathing," my mind tells me. This movement of the lungs, whether I am aware of it or not, goes on because of involuntary impulses from what physiologists refer to as the autonomic nervous system. Without this breathing all the processes of my feeling and thinking would cease. And its effortlessness suggests that it is the end product of aeons of infinitely slow, irresistible evolution. These lungs and the mechanism that works them are an integral part of my subjective environment, just as the whole of the physical body is. And yet, though I may associate them with the self, they, too, are not what I really mean when I speak of "I" or "me. They are vital to me, but by thinking them to be the self I cannot achieve the at-homeness with the elements of my immediate inner environment that I seek.

Next, as I continue to watch myself and consciously experience myself, I sense the beating of my heart. This is not so immediately evident as breathing, but it derives from an even more primordial stage, perhaps, of our physical evolution. Without its basic rhythmic motion—reminding one of the pulsing of waves on the seashore—the blood could not feed my system. It is that motion which enables the blood coming from my extremities and organs to enter the right auricle (or receiving pumping chamber) and from there pass into the right ventricle (or delivery chamber), which sends it to the lungs. The lungs then return it to the left auricle and ventricle, to pass it out again to the organs and the extremities. And this blood is a true continuation of the salt-sea environment from which my life and all earthly life originally sprang. This heart and this blood are also an integral part of my subjective environment. And yet, though I associate them, too, with the self, they, too, are not what I really mean when I speak of "I" or "me."

Turning the mind, now, more deeply, I become aware of the activities of uncurbed thought. The flow of thought has its origins far back beyond the limits of recorded history; eventually it became staggeringly elaborate. This uncurbed thought, a form of energy, would be impossible without the presence of an infinitely complex system of neurons, or nerve cells, in the brain, all depending on the continuing action of lungs and heart. It may take the form (when, as in the present situation, I sit to observe myself) of a seemingly endless wandering, something like the activity of the dream mind—though often even more whimsical. Or it may take the form of memories, or of logical analysis of other thinking, or of aesthetic or passional reaction to previous or present sense impressions. It is, in fact, almost inexhaustible in its variety. All forms of thought are an integral part of my subjective environment. And yet though I associate them perhaps even more intimately than these other elements with the self, they, too, are not what I really mean when I speak of "I" or "me." I am their observer and in that sense they become objects.

When I open my eyes and return to the world of the self as I come upon it face to face in everyday waking experience, I am in touch with not only an inner world but a world reported by all five senses: hearing, touch, sight, taste, and smell. The miracle of sense perception, too, is the result of a long evolutionary history. With it, perhaps, first arose the seed of ego: not only the thought "I am thus-and-so," but "I am feeling thus-and-so." If I look at my everyday waking experience with unbiased mind, however, I note that it is only when I *think about* perception (as about thought itself) that a sense of separate ego appears: "I am hearing," "I am seeing," and so on. When I experience the objects of the senses to the utmost of my capacity—that is to say, with full attention—there is no awareness of separate ego. The ego, which thus comes and goes, can hardly be what I mean by "I" or "me."

When I say, "I am tall," "I am short," "I am fat," the implication is that the self is the body. When I say, "I am happy," "I am sad," "I am hungry," the implication is that the self is the mind. But it is actually in terms of ego that I am speaking here, which, to speak accurately, arises as a thought at the same time as the thought of tallness or happiness or the rest. In both instances I am confusing the ego-self with the person. Speaking in terms of ego (which, if the truth be told, is merely a useful mythological fiction), I may say that the ego is part of the person. True enough, the *I* in the statement "I am tall" or "I am happy" may be thus considered as being included in the person. But the true self or true *I* we are seeking to identify, though associated with it, is not included in the person as being subordinate to it. For it is *aware* of the changing states of the person.

What is said in the two preceding paragraphs, as indeed in those earlier ones dealing with the body, the lungs, the heart, the mind, may of course be said equally well of all the parallel experiences in dreams.

We must conclude that the self is not to be identified with any one of those aspects of the person it is usually identified with under the guise of ego. It is not identical with the body or the breathing or the heartbeat, or with the flow of thought or with ego, any more than it is to be identified with the various sheaths said by Hindus to be associated with it, or the knowledge, thinking, feeling, and willing said by Christians to characterize it, or with the several layers of consciousness said by psychoanalysts to compose it. And yet it is not completely independent of them, either. Its relationship to all these elements of the person is what we may call—to borrow a phrase coined by certain Hindu devotional mystics to describe the soul's relation to God—one of "incomprehensible difference in identity."

Who then is this self? What is it? Where is it to be found? After having listed all that it is not, perhaps one might expect something spectacular in the way of revelation about it. All I can offer is a few very unspectacular statements—stemming directly from our negations. Even these statements I make only with the proviso that the "me" we are talking about is the "me" that as true subject is a direct *experience;* none of them makes sense if we let them suggest that the "me" is simply another object of thought.

Who the self is, we know directly: it is that which we intuitively grasp as our absolute essence, whether we recognize its presence consciously or not. It is the something—the someone—who *is* the core experiences "I am," "I am aware," and "I love" (in their most rigorous sense). That is all we can say positively.

What the self is, we cannot hope to conceive intellectually, because (except when abstractly thought about) this something/someone, as already pointed out, is not an object. If we speak in terms of its functions, we may venture to call it the creative focus of thought-energy and feeling-energy in each of us. Little else can be said about what it is except that without it we could not be. It is a mystery—like all spiritual mysteries, dark only because of utter simplicity.

Where the self is, provides some interesting food for thought. We have noted the self 's—like the sun's—nowness. We have also noted the fact that the sun, from its own point of view, is always at noon, always "right here," while we on earth go turning away from its noon and back again. In another sense, we, as the self, are always "right here," too. As the creative focus of all the thought-energy and feeling-energy known to each of us, there is nothing more evidently "here" for us than the self. (This is said, of course, in terms of its relation to the body and mind, which we saw to be one of "incomprehensible difference in identity.") That fact explains perhaps why where *we* are always seems to us to be stationary and why the sun seems to be moving—even when we know intellectually that the appearance is caused by optical illusion. Here we can see the justice in saying that the self is both intimately related to the body and its functions and yet not identical with them. For while physically we *are* moving away from the sun and back again, each twenty-four hours, psychically we are as unmoving as the sun.

This thought may be an unfamiliar one and may seem a bit odd or difficult. But if we stop to think about it, we can see that though thought and feeling *appear* to be enclosed in the body, they are not related to space in the way that physical objects are. In terms of the self as the creative focus of thought-energy and feeling-energy, we can also truly speak of a "here," for all those thoughts and feelings of ours belong in the world of the self. If we want to play with words, we may speak of the *where* of the self as a *no-where* that is also *now-here*.

Does all this mean there is no hope of our becoming more familiar with the self than we now are? Quite the contrary. Once arrived at consciously, intuitive knowledge has its own way of revealing truths beyond the grasp of the intellect. It is perfectly possible for normal men and women to learn to participate more fully in the core experiences "I am," "I am aware," and "I love" without grasping them intellectually—until they become more acutely aware of the self's presence, and thus more alert to whatever aspect of the total inner environment presents itself at any moment. Some persons otherwise quite average appear to be gifted with such a capacity by nature. Others may come to possess it after an amount of effort.

Even after having intuitively made contact with the self, one is by no means assured of continuous participation. Whenever it is dimmed, awareness of the self as central presence may be restored by mentally withdrawing the five senses from all sides, and letting it reaffirm itself directly—though, again, not so as to appear an object of thought. If awareness of the self's mystery is completely clouded over, one may remind oneself of its incomprehensible relationship with the body by studying the body from the toes to the crown of the head.

When we open ourselves to the self in everyday life, even to a slight degree, a new phase in mental life begins. We come to understand the paramount function it performs for body and soul. Slowly we come to see it, like the sun, as a living reality. It too then becomes for us a stepping-off place—this time into the fathomless space of thought. Just as I have with the sun, in the past few years I have felt a strong urge to intensify my own acquaintance with the self. The result is a fresh sense of relatedness both to the world within me and to the world within others.

To manage all this, exercise of will is needed. One must train the mind so that, whenever legitimate practical concerns do not occupy it, it returns to attentive awareness of the self.

* * *

Unlike the sun, the human self we are speaking of was never popularly worshiped as a symbol of divine energy. Indeed, it was hardly thought about at all by most people. Ancient Hindu sages were possibly the first to note that we humans, in our preoccupation with the physical world, neglect what is nearest to each one of us. As a famous Hindu scripture puts it:

> The self-existent Supreme Lord inflicted an injury upon the sense-organs, when he created them, in causing them to turn outward; Therefore a man perceives outer objects with them, and not the inner self.

True, the Vedic sages turned their attention to it, as later Hindu psychologists did, and by concentrating on it made a breakthrough to realize the Oversoul, or Atman, which enlightens it. But having found something that appeared to them ultimately real (by which they also meant unchanging), they understandably never emphasized the inexhaustible but seemingly less ultimate divine energy manifested through the individual human self. Had they foreseen the consequences for average men and women, they might have laid stress on this very present witness to the power that sustains the universe and everything in it.

It is not a question, then, of urging a *return* (as with the sun) to recognition of the self as an expression of the divine, but rather of initially proposing such recognition. For the self is not just a peculiarly apt symbol of the whole subjective world within the human person. As the "image" of God it has, so to speak, created that subjective world. In seeking to turn our attention toward the self, we are not seeking like mystics to go to God or ultimate reality *through* the self but rather, as already indicated, to find a manifestation of creative power *in* the self. This is not to deny that there is something beyond the self. But we have to become aware that as vehicle for the "true light that enlightens every man," the self is, like the sun, not unrelated to ultimate reality.

In a sense, the self creates each person's individual reading of the physical world. No one individual sees a perfectly objective world identical in each detail with that seen by others. Each person's world is qualified by his or her past experiences and present preferences. But one has to assume that one is seeing a world that roughly corresponds with what others see (in fact, almost all of us uncritically assume that we are seeing the *same* world). No doubt there is, as most of us confidently assume, a noumenal "x" behind the phenomenal world, but this "x" is by no stretch of imagination the actual world that each of us sees and takes part in. Matter, it has been said, is the "permanent possibility of sensation." Perhaps that is as near as we can come to a description of our physical environment—besides one in terms of atoms and atomic particles—as it exists beyond our individual minds. This is not to deny that there may be, in the collective unconscious, some general world pattern on which our separate interpretations of the phenomenal world are based. But whatever may be the case, it is the individual self that integrates each person's sense impressions into a coherent interpretation of that pattern.

Just as the self could not, from the point of view of evolution, have become manifest without the sun's presence, so, from the point of view of our nowness, without the self the sun's presence would remain unknown. Had no person and no self-awareness emerged, had consciousness developed only to the stage we conjecture it has in animals, there could never have emerged the complete awareness-of-others that illuminates the consciousness we now possess. From our human point of view, we may presume to say that our self, or true *I,* is as important for us not only as any other self, but as the sun is. For our own self, as surely as the sun, is a bringer of light and life to the obscure night of matter and the animal mind. Though we do all we can to ignore the fact, we are all of us in daily, continuous, communion with the wellspring of the life that is our being.

The curious relationship of the world of the self and the world of the sun parallels this relationship of self and sun, and actually points to the necessity of a noumenal "x." Thinking along these lines, one may perhaps be tempted to regard the phenomenal world one sees as entirely the product of the mind working through the brain. Each particular object one sees is known to exist only through the mind, and is colored and interpreted in relation to one's own memory. Yet, as that same mind has to admit, the brain can function only by grace of nutrients derived from outside it. (The brain may be said, from the point of view of another, to belong to the outside physical world, but it cannot observe *itself* as a part of that world.) And without the instrumentality of the brain the mind cannot build up a personal apprehension of the physical world. Thus it is driven to accept the existence of a reality underlying that world to escape being imprisoned in solipsistic thinking.

COUNTERPOISE

The measured thunder of your heart
Reverberates among the stars,
The straining rivers of your blood
Inseminate the hemispheres:
Without their rhythmical supply,
This universe your brain has built
Would fade to blankest nothingness
And all its shining flicker out.

And yet these rivers that support
Your heavens and your hemispheres,
Starved of sufficient food and air
Would slacken, too, to nothingness.
How neat the ancient counterpoise:
Each by the other's stuff upheld—
Without the nurturing world, no blood,
Without the fathering blood, no world.

The self is the direct source of all the psychological creative power humans can know outside faith or mystical experience, and indeed the source of the interpretive power that fashions for each human being a universe according to his or her own lights. In its own way—as we cannot remind ourselves too often—the self is, like the sun, a true showing forth of elemental creative energy.

The self, dazzlingly dark within each of us, can be, when intuitively grasped, a source of aesthetic and spiritual refreshment just as potent as the sight of the blazing sun. If the sun can appear as a song of affirmation to the cosmic energy, the self can appear —for those who have ears to hear—as a hymn to the inexhaustible microcosmic energy within each human being. When we look at it with the inward eye of the mind, we are looking, even more clearly than when we look at the sun, at humankind's past development as a species and its future potentiality as a community of spirits. Just as we naively experience it, it shines as the naked face of psychological reality.

Our behavior toward the self is quite as understandable as our behavior toward the sun, but even less justifiable. We have utterly refused appreciation, reverence, and love to the immediate cause of our awareness of the whole spectrum of human achievements: physical, mental, spiritual. In this refusal, we have maimed our spirituality perhaps more than in cutting ourselves off from the sun. For in refusing consciously to *be* and *be aware of* the self, we have opened ourselves to danger greater than ever we did in allowing ourselves to become the slaves of concepts about and symbols of God received second hand. We have come to think of the self as a mere object and securely walled ourselves away from the something beyond toward which it points. In thus losing sight of what transcends thought and feeling and speech, we have undoubtedly lost sight of our total meaning as humans.

Perhaps the danger to the sense of human community that indifference to the self entails is graver, too, than the danger inherent in indifference to the sun. Our unspoken but nonetheless real alienation from one another as persons stems in large part from this alienation of ours from the self. I am not urging a plunge into meditation on an Oversoul within: I am simply urging that we should come to know our surface world of the self in all its unrecognized splendor. In this way we should restore the balance in our thinking between our own inner world and the inner world of others. And thus learn to see through others' eyes, feel through others' emotions, think through others' minds, and so redeem our sense of belonging to one another.

Those religiously minded persons who feel spiritually under-nourished in today's world would not be the only ones to benefit from such a readjustment of attention. Nonbelievers could also find an appropriate focus for attentiveness and a fertile source of respectful appreciation in the self. By becoming alert to it they would begin to feel gratitude for this undeniably vital aspect of the inner environment—and to wonder at the subtle chance that allowed it to manifest itself at the end of humanity's physical and sensate evolution. They, no less than religious believers, could fill up the void they unknowingly harbor in themselves by according it their gratitude as a measure of their appreciation. To do so would be an excellent way for any human being to begin paying off his or her debt to the psychological environment symbolized by the self.

* * *

Like the sun, the self is a peculiarly apt symbol for its world just because it, too, is really more than a symbol. It should be clear by now that it *is* our inner environment in quite as real a sense as the sun is our outer environment. We can never sufficiently impress upon ourselves what it means to us. For the whole of our psychological surroundings, every aspect of our subjective Now, depends (for each of us) on the self and its near presence. Our thought-life system owes to this living focus—this delicately responsive fountainhead of furiously active thoughts and feelings and intuitions for which our nerve cells in the brain and nerve currents in the body are the vehicles—not only its short span of development within our body. It owes to it, too, the present and continuing existence (as illuminated by the self) of everything it allows us to perceive as living and moving and reproducing within our whole area of apprehension. All this becomes clear once our relationship to the self is established in experience.

Our own personal knowledge of the positioning and chemical structure of the earth, of the presence of the conditions necessary for the emergence of life, owes its existence to the self. Our personal knowledge of the characteristics of microorganisms and plants, of fish and other aquatic creatures, of insects, reptiles, birds, mammals, and of the evolution that brought them into being—all this could arrange itself in our thinking only because of the presence and perfect "positioning" of the self. And no less our personal knowledge of the whole tremendous phenomenon of the development of human beings and human consciousness.

As with our inattention to the sun, our very want of attentiveness to the self is a tribute to its all-importance for us. The fact that we take it for granted may indicate better than any words its ultimacy, its immediacy, so far as we are concerned. We cannot say, in the present instance, that this sort of tribute of indifference is more appropriate for other living beings, because (so we believe) we humans are the only ones on earth that are or can be fully aware of a self. Why most men and women, ancient or modern, have steered clear of much thinking about the self or true *I* may be no mystery. Thought *about* the self usually assumes that the thinking self is quite different from the self thought about. And so it makes a caricature of experience in elevating what should disappear—the sense of a separate, self-sufficient ego-self—into an all-important something that is really only another form of thought.

"I am aware," "I am," and "I love": this is the nearest we can get to the self. Though familiarity with the self is what we are trying to arrive at, there is always a danger of identifying it merely with the ego-self, which too easily says, "I am happy," "I know this or that," "I love so-and-so." We have to be content to accept the fact that the self *is*, without making it an object of thought. No one is foolish enough to try to see his own face directly.

It was perhaps a healthy, normal urge that persuaded ordinary men and women in the past to mistrust those who sought out the self—quite as much as they mistrusted those who would look directly at the sun. Yet now that so many humans have come close to the fullest development of the psyche possible in our stage of evolution, it may be time for the healthy, normal man or woman to abandon such mistrust.

This self, not analyzed intellectually but knowingly participated in, is—like the sun itself—one of the most arresting of wonders. Alertness to it brings us one step farther on our way to being at home with our total environment and so to becoming more fully human. If we can open ourselves to it in this more intimate sense, through simple awareness of our continuous participation in it, we should be on the way to a new mutation in consciousness.

For in the end we find that living in the self puts us in touch with the world outside us and the world within us in an unexpected manner. The locus of the self, we find, is not only a *no-where* that is *now-here*, but a *no-where* that is *every-where*. Strange, one says to oneself, that no one, either among the ancients or the moderns, has imputed to this human self the divine characteristics the ancients imputed to the sun.

* * *

Exploration of the reaches of "inner space" is the privilege of every man or woman who wants to become at home in it. Once we have attained a measure of openness to the self, the mind is no longer a forbidden area. All the gradations of emotion, positive and negative; all the variety of intellectual thinking, logical and illogical, and all the instantaneous reactions to sense impressions become familiar landmarks—no longer strange shapes come upon unexpectedly. We can observe our tendencies toward depression or elation, toward self-confidence or undue self-depreciation, toward generosity or miserliness, toward habitual comparison of ourselves with others or imitation of others, and come to understand how seriously to take them. If we lose our sense of focus or become mentally exhausted, we can learn to rest the mind by forcefully distracting it and turning it away from exaggerated feelings or reasonings. After a time we can even detect telltale signs of the stirring of emotions, thoughts, or desires that if not checked may overpower the mind at some future time. Above all, we can learn to watch objectively the inexhaustible flow of the ego-thought instead of compulsively identifying ourselves with it.

By watching our reactions when reading or when listening to a lecture, we can discover whether our mind is predominantly visual or aural or tactile (how well it re-creates the scenes described in terms of sights, sounds, touches, and the like). We can amuse ourselves by observing how the mind deals with certain groups of facts that are constantly to be kept in the background of our thought: how, for example, it pictures to itself the hours of the day, the days of the month, the months of the year, the years of the centuries, the millennia before and after Christ—and so on. I myself picture the months as if they were on the face of a clock, and the nineteenth century must have a special meaning for me for it alone, of all the centuries, occupies a well-defined linear stretch with the American Civil War and the spiritual struggles of Ramakrishna in the middle. On speaking to an eighteen-year-old girl of my acquaintance, I discovered that she associated the days of the week with certain people, and quite as curiously, that her younger sister associated them with colors: Sunday with green, Monday with brown, Tuesday with violet, and so on. There is no end of opportunities, for those who care to know their minds better, to explore their own inner space and make it their own. The change in perspective to be achieved by any person, if he or she becomes a self-trained "astronaut" in the inner cosmos of thought, not only expands the mind but makes it more fully human.

To open oneself gradually to the self does more than provide a stepping-off place into a wider world of thought and feeling. As already noted, it opens a door to closer intimacy with other selves on earth, to an affectionate and respectful (and sometimes compassionate) relationship with them based on awareness of the interdependence of all humans. Others can know us, as we can know others, only to the extent that both of us know *ourselves.* The more successfully we have learned to participate intuitively in the self, the easier it will be to grasp what another human being is in his or her person and so meet that other human unswayed by irrelevant imaginings or by prejudgments about intrinsic virtues or shortcomings. Since trying to intensify my own awareness of my relationship to the self, and so to the world it sustains, I can personally attest to a new feeling of closeness to most of the people I encounter.

One of the first effects one experiences after achieving an increased attentiveness to the self is an increase of goodwill toward others. This quality was, I think, partly developed in my own case before I became aware of the value of attentiveness to the self and its world. But since I already had a natural inclination to explore both of them, I also think it is fair to attribute it to the same cause. More striking, perhaps, is an intensified wish to remember daily and put oneself (in thought) in the presence of the various friends who have contributed to one's well-being and mean much to one. It is pointless, I came to realize, to "keep up" friendships and yet hardly think of the absent friends except when they happen to write letters or make long-distance telephone calls. This applies equally to friends and valued relatives who have died. A similar recognition of one's debt of gratitude makes itself felt toward great figures of history—artists, scientists, literary figures, musicians, saints, and so on—who have made one's life richer. One comes also to make a practice of daily asking forgiveness, mentally, of anyone whom one has thoughtlessly disregarded or looked down upon or wished ill to during the preceding day.

Most important of all for me is the development of an increased understanding that all the people I meet and form opinions of are self-oriented persons with all-absorbing concerns of their own. They are not here simply as occasions for my receiving their attention, or as an audience for my ideas. By nature they are all intimately related to me. And if I am ever to relate properly to them, I must realize that they are to be "approached from within." This involves a willingness to refrain from judging them —and a recognition that what one heartily disapproves of in another is a rather good index of the same failings in oneself that one is still unwilling to face. Instead of being shocked when I see behind the façade they present to the world or that I imagine them to have, I try (not always consistently) to grasp why they are as they are. And in trying to do this, I learn also that the only way to ensure others' peace of mind when they discover what I myself am like inside is to *be* inside what I appear to be outside. (This is a goal that I believe should be slowly realized as a natural outcome of one's thinking. There is no need to strain unnaturally to be better than one as yet knows how to be before one's emotions and impulses have caught up with one's best thinking.)

A central secret of approaching others successfully is to meet everyone on his or her own level, without condescension and without abandoning one's own best instincts. This happens spontaneously, I believe, as one becomes more and more at home with the world of the self. When we are with a three-year-old, for instance, we then forget our own age and become (more or less!) as a three-year-old. When we are with people younger than ourselves, we think as far as possible along with them, share their sincerities and enthusiasms, forget to feel (except where absolutely necessary) that we are older and more experienced than they are. Again, when with those of our own age or with older persons, we remain our own age. We can hardly become "older" when someone is much older than ourselves! (I myself find that sometimes I actually assume that a person younger than myself, but with maturer understanding or greater experience, is older than I am.) None of all this need be attempted consciously.

As we come to know ourselves better, it is also possible to meet each stranger we encounter during the day as a friend and, so far as propriety allows, not wait for closer acquaintance to open ourselves to him or her on matters of ordinary concern. If we approach each person as another self-oriented being, the response we receive is amazing. The habit of meeting others on their own level is, of course, the secret of meaningful relationships with animals and other "lower" creatures.

Related to this whole subject is the capacity one may develop for forming close relationships with persons unrelated by blood. This is a natural characteristic of very many people in India, and possibly of many others in the East. A first revealing experience of this sort was my being quietly adopted as a "son" by one of the most high-minded and gifted Hindus I have been privileged to know. I met Chandicharan Palit, a retired professor of chemistry, in Allahabad on a visit to India in 1949. From our first meeting we were drawn to each other and before I left India we knew we were father and son. For twenty years thereafter we were in touch by correspondence, and we met again in 1959 and 1968, on each occasion with deep satisfaction and joy. When in 1969 my adopted father died, my sense of loss was as profound as any I have known. So complete was the relationship that his two sons, many years my junior, accepted me and deferred to me as their older brother.

I recently discovered a "son" of my own in Sri Lanka. Piyaratna Wanigatunga, a taximan and travel guide whom I first met in 1970, adopted me as his "Papa." When I returned in 1973, he took me home to meet his family. His intelligence and resourcefulness had drawn my attention from the start, and it was quite natural to look on this young man in his early thirties with more than casual affection. Even today I still receive a letter from him every month. His respect and concern for my welfare have taught me what it is to be proud of a son, though I never had one in the flesh. These are only two oustanding examples of close friends with whom a relationship has developed beyond the ordinary bounds of friendship.

As a result of increased attentiveness to the self (in others as well as oneself), we may also find we have been adopted as a family member by families other than our own so that there is no need to be formal about asking to stay with them when we plan to visit their town or their country. Another, and very happy, aspect of this sort of relationship is finding that one's own blood brothers or sisters have become honored friends rather than remaining mere flesh-and-blood relatives not of one's own choosing. It is possible, I believe, to learn how to make our daily meetings with members of our own family or with coworkers or social acquaintances as interestingly fresh as encounters with total strangers. These are only a few of the interpersonal relationships that, while possible perhaps without diligent attentiveness to the self, may be enriched through it.

There is another side to at-homeness with the self in relation to the world around one. This is something that transcends individual relationships and yet may be the basis for all of them. I speak of it only on the evidence of certain poetic moods where intuition of the self's meaning has been especially strong. In such states there is an intense identification with the whole of the inner environment and an equally intense identification of that inner world with the whole of the outer world. As with similar states connected more particularly with the world of the sun, it is impossible to convey more than a hint of what this experience is. Until one has made the effort to know the self, or has been allowed to open oneself to it through the grace of circumstances, one may not fully understand. Nevertheless, there is something of the poet in almost everyone and it is not completely meaningless to try to express what such a mood involves.

LOOKING SEAWARD

I am in all created things,
Present or past or yet to be—
Whether as essence or as occasion
Of their immediacy:
Water and sky and cloud and gull,
Passage of storm, pause of lull,
All I can think of or can see
Thronging without or inwardly,
All that creation can invent

Of function, form, or element,
Are interfused with me.

What wonder, then, that I should cling
To shoreward ways for anchoring,
Should stow my secret deep,
When the full splendor of the thing
Would carry seaward in its sweep
The shreds of my identity;
And for appearance' sake profess,
While still I tend upon the shore
The tasks of shoreward busyness,
To favor some a little more
And some a little less.

In cultivating our personal relationship with the self—source of our mental life and illuminator of not only our thought-world but our world of physical matter—we can look forward to all this, and indeed to far more. To take the self for symbol of our inner environment is no more of a poetic whim than to take the sun for symbol of what lies around us. As we fix attention on them ever more alertly, the myriad details of the world of the self that rise to meet us become increasingly meaningful until, as with those we encounter in the outer world, we achieve a devoted attentiveness to all of them sufficient to open our insight to further vistas of understanding.

* * *

As with the sun, here, too, with the self: to come nearer to full and continuous awareness of our relationship to it and to the world it symbolizes, we have in theory to achieve a constantly available sense of its presence. Except in the most unusual instances, such a realization can become ours only through unflagging effort. For the realization itself, even when achieved, is something that, until fully established, fades without daily practice.

This sort of effort, we are told, is possible only for those to whom precious hours for meditation are available completely free from interruption. Here, again, I must beg to differ. Unflagging effort is indeed necessary, but for most of us it need not be heroically strenuous. Average men and women need only adopt means within their grasp and remain content with a gradually intensified awareness of the self's presence and of the fathomless world it supports. Only let their dissatisfaction with their present state of understanding persist, whether on the conscious or a subliminal level. They may then confidently look forward to an eventual awareness of the self that will, like the self itself, not fail them but enliven them and refresh them with self-perpetuating vision. Achieving this more relaxed approach has been our chief concern in this second stage of our journey.

The sun and the self do indeed symbolize for us the first two aspects of our environment. But they suffer from a peculiar limitation when we look at them as separate entities instead of experiencing them and their worlds immediately, as an indivisible whole. However much we may talk about taking part in the objective or subjective world, we are still dealing in abstractions: so long as the world remains divided for us, in thought, into object and subject, we are experiencing it only piecemeal. We are not experiencing it as the seamless whole it actually is. If we are to know these aspects of our environment as they are, that is to say, unabstractly and not as objects of thought, we must become alert to a third factor. For it is this factor that confers actuality on our environment, outer and inner.

✴ THE NOW OF SPIRIT

PRESENCE

Between me and the moving world's
Variable play of light and sound
You intervene, not less revealed
Because too instant to be known.

Between me and my clearest thought,
My fiercest love, my closest prayer,
Still you contrive to penetrate:
The crux of now, the core of here.

Though I could cross creation out,
Dissolve all elements in one,
Your presence would unvarying wait
Where, from forever, it has been

The silent mover of the play,
The focus of its myriad parts—
Fashioning, for the world and me,
A wholeness from our opposites.

By the time I graduated from college, I must have known that
spirit was more than a vaguely sensed life principle or ani-
mating force somehow related to oneself and to the world in
general. Even so, I hardly thought of it in terms of personal
experience, let alone made any conscious effort to realize its
immediate presence. Looking farther back, though, into boyhood, I recall a repeated happening that was closely related to the
working of spirit. Beginning as a sort of aesthetic addiction, it led

to something beyond the world of the senses. Perhaps the most natural way to think of it is as an extreme example of the sort of fusing of inner perceiver with the object perceived that I dwelt on in the prologue as seeming to represent the working of spirit. For those not used to thinking of spirit in terms of experience, it may prove to be a useful handle. Just because its culmination was not a conscious mystical breakthrough, it may reveal something about the third aspect of our environment that most of us may not appreciate: that experience of the presence of spirit is not necessarily limited to saints or yogis or Zen monks.

When I was nine years old our family acquired a summer place in the country, situated at the top of a small, oak-clad hill. As a result of my father's example I already felt at home in the outdoors, but now I was continuously exposed to the natural world. Not only could I roam about the woods and fields and streams, and become friendly with the sun; I could also turn my attention to the myriad different devisings of nature throughout each day of summer. One of these completely captured my fancy: the cloudless sky from immediately after sundown to just before nightfall.

The sway that the sky after sundown exercised over me was an unusual one. The sheer expanse of deep, radiant blue held me spellbound; often I watched it unswervingly until most of the light had faded, entertaining no other thought. On days that promised a cloudless sky, whenever I could I disengaged myself from the family just before the sun disappeared. I would hurry out to the west end of our hilltop, down a stretch of grass between perennial borders, and spend long minutes gazing at the sky's perfection. To claim my complete attention it had to be free of the slightest distracting detail. A single wisp of cloud turned burning gold by the now invisible sun, beautiful though it was, was enough to break the flow of an almost devout attentiveness. Without knowing it, I was making use of a potent wakener of spirit—as the tranquillity that possessed my mind for some time after bore witness. It was not the sky simply as an object that I was fixing my attention on, as when I had earlier looked at the sun. Perhaps the habit started that way; but I soon was using the

flawless, glowing evening sky as a means to direct the mind
beyond the sky, to something undefined and undefinable.

This aesthetic addiction continued for many years, perhaps
until I was fifteen, and I never spoke of it to any member of the
family. On one particular evening, perhaps the last time I looked
at the sky with complete attentiveness, the experience passed
beyond ordinary aesthetic enjoyment or even the sense of something undefined. I had begun to watch the cloudless sky as usual,
standing near a summerhouse covered with profusely blooming,
delicate pink climbing roses. I stood there for some time.
. . . When I came to myself, twilight had deepened into dusk. I
could hardly see the roses. Only then did I realize that something
new had happened. For all that time I was utterly lost to the world
around me and within me.

Perhaps the experience, whatever else it meant, provided a
faint poetic foreshadowing of a degree of contemplation
achieved after intense effort by certain contemplatives. The one
thing sure about it is that I entered into it after a short period of
one-pointed attentiveness. But, as already noted, my attention
had not been directed to a definite object of perception, as when
I looked at the sun. Nor had it been directed to an inner process
of the mind, as later when I practiced the Hindu breathing exercises. The experience was accompanied neither by the precise
objective awareness of the first example, nor by the persuasive
inwardness of the second. Here the aesthetic contemplation of
undifferentiated and slowly fading color and light appears to
have withdrawn the mind temporarily from conscious contact
with both physical world and psychological world, so that it
became passively absorbed in an obscure oneness.

I cannot recall the content of those moments of absentness,
and indeed could not do so immediately afterwards. Yet the
experience was not a blank: the sense of its having had positive
content still remains. Possibly it gives a hint of the mystical sense
of the Void mentioned not only by Zen masters but by a few early
mystics of the Christian church who spoke of knowing God
through "unknowing." At least it has made their descriptions of
that type of experience less difficult to penetrate.

A poem written many years after, though not directly referring to this particular experience, could never have been composed without the memory of my addiction to the cloudless evening sky—and of that strange period of abstraction.

CLEAR EVENING

Across the beach of sky
Night's imperceptible flow
Filters its sure way—
Deceiving in that while
Its depth increases, still
Some glimmer from beneath
Keeps on shining through,
So that as long as you
Watch only in one place
No change seems to occur,
And, before you know,
The tide has filtered quite
Across that dry expanse
And reaches for the shell
Of new moon that lies there
Half hidden in blue sands,
When, having risen and flowed
Even to the burnt orange
Mainland of the west,
It wraps all else from view:
Only that shell persists,
Increasingly intense
Under night's flood tide,
And a few starfish glints
Scattered near about,
To hint the beach it hides.

Was this indeed a faint foretaste of spirit perceived as underlying the physical and mental worlds? If it was, it came without conscious preparation. Still, the experience had been preceded by a long series of attentive contemplations such as someone might have undertaken if seeking to obtain that sort of revelation.

More clearly related to the working of spirit has been another repeated experience of mine. The phenomenon that accompanies the conceiving and birth of a live poem is something known to creative artists in general, and to poets and musical composers in particular—more especially those of an earlier time. It is often referred to by the currently unfashionable term "inspiration." Faintly sensed on some occasions, it can be almost overpoweringly real on others. One well-known poet has called it, a bit melodramatically, the "poetic trance." It is a state of mind that involves awareness of the immediate presence of spirit more clearly than does either the fusing of the inner perceiver with perceived objects of sense or thought, or the experience of their complete withdrawal as when I was rapt in contemplation of the evening sky.

During this poetic experience both object and inner perceiver remain in consciousness. In addition to a heightened sensitivity to oneself and to one's surroundings, what characterizes such a state is a flow of ideas, often seemingly new, or newly understood. As it intensifies, a preoccupation with words to express the ideas may temporarily block out distinct awareness of anything else. Frequently the poet visited by this state of mind does not know what subject he or she will write on when it first arrives. The materials are furnished from somewhere within the person— perhaps from the preconscious layer of the mind, as Freud might call it. I say this because on surprisingly many occasions a poem has occurred to me very nearly in the form it finally assumed. I believe that the revealing and organizing of such poems may be interpreted as the creative work of spirit. Such a state of mind may produce a single poem or several poems.

I have not asked friends of mine who are poets about the frequency of their inspirations. As for myself, I have known not only inspirations that resulted in the writing of a number of poems in one day, but a few creative periods that lasted intermittently for weeks or even months. In the summer of 1944, for instance, perhaps partly as a result of my first stimulating contact with D. T. Suzuki's pioneering works on Zen, eighty poems were given to me almost fully formed, and of nearly uniform quality, in the same number of days. In 1951, again, after a renewed acquaintance with Emily Dickinson's work, there occurred an eruption of sixty-five poems in sixty days—this time of uneven quality. The most memorable example of such an invasion was in 1956, when in the course of a year about 275 poems of extremely varied subject matter and quality were given to me— among them, I think, some successful poems. And these were followed, in 1957, by 115 more. All this in addition to the normal flow, between times, of single poems that, except in dry spells, a poet normally receives.

Long before I formed the idea of writing this present book, poems about the sun and the self, and about spirit, had occurred to me. And many of them would fit into no collection until the book began to form. During its composition, a flood of ideas from time to time poured into my mind, as if they had been stored up for years and were simply waiting to be released. One poem I conceived in a creative period more than twenty-five years back gives lively expression to an intuition about spirit. It is the poem "Presence" quoted at the start of this chapter, which in all probability prompted my first working plan for the book. What it shows rather clearly is that when we speak of spirit—even as here through poetic intuition—we have to use terms that are approximate and ultimately inadequate. And yet the poet's assumption that one *can* legitimately speak in these terms suggests a confidence that all of us, and not merely professed mystics, may well be able to achieve more than a poetic intuition about spirit.

When we approach spirit even in this inadequate and somewhat intellectualized way, our conception of it becomes the key to a far-reaching awareness. The vision of a twofold world—of perceiving "me" and world perceived—made one through spirit, serves as a stepping-off place into a cosmos of boundless and unceasing creativity, centered now and here. Such awareness still requires, however, translation into a conscious continuing realization of immediate presence. As we have seen in the prologue, such an awareness is stimulated by the practice of attentiveness to the sun and the self. But once possessed of some measure of it, we can refine and intensify our sense of spirit's presence, as well, by familiarizing ourselves with others' witness to spirit.

* * *

In giving our attention to what spiritually sophisticated persons have said about spirit, we accomplish two results. We gradually increase our at-homeness with the idea of spirit as an aspect of our environment. We also prepare the ground for *recognizing* its immediate presence when finally we are ready to participate in it consciously. A brief look at some details of the Judeo-Christian and Hindu insights about spirit will be useful here.

Both in the Old Testament and in the New, terms are used that suggest our idea of spirit. From very early times the Jews conceived of a creative spirit immediately in touch with them and deeply involved in their world. The term they used was *spirit of God.* The most important meaning given to the term in the Old Testament is that of God acting in human beings and in the universe. "When God began to create the heavens and the earth . . . the spirit of God was moving over the face of the waters"— that is how the creative action is described in the Hebrew of the First Book of Moses, or Genesis. The Book of Job speaks of the spirit of God as creating the human soul, and of the "breath of the Almighty" as giving it life, that is to say, sustaining its existence.

The spirit of God is also seen to be at work in the gift of prophecy that the Jews recognized as manifested throughout much of their history in their outstanding spiritual leaders, the prophets. A further extension of the spirit's creative working is seen in the gift of divine inspiration. The authors who set down the thirty-nine canonical books of the Old Testament were supposed by the Jews to have been inspired in a special sense. God, acting through them, was thought to have revealed the divine nature in these books for their special guidance. The process by which their composition was accomplished is surely not very different from that by which musicians, poets, and other artists have created their noblest works throughout history.

The first Christians, being Jews, naturally preserved the concept of the spirit of God. The term they used is *Holy Spirit,* but its reference seems identical to that of the earlier term. Much of the recorded life of Jesus is couched in terms of the Holy Spirit. Conceived, it was believed, through the Spirit's intervention, he is said also to have received the Spirit at the moment of baptism. During his active life he spoke of the Holy Spirit in various connections. The Apostles spoke of the Spirit even more frequently.

For the Apostles, the most significant experience of the Holy Spirit came after Jesus' death, when it is said to have descended on them at Pentecost. Peter interprets this happening, when the Apostles were able to speak intelligibly to people of many nations, as fulfillment of God's promise in the Old Testament to "pour out" the spirit "on all flesh." In Peter's view it was the same spirit of God at work in his day among Christians that had been at work hitherto among Jews to bring them to God. From then on, most Christians believe, the Holy Spirit has been not only their church's animator but the evolutionary force that impels it, and through it the whole of history, to fulfillment. Many Christians, holding that the church is potentially the whole of humanity, suggest that Christ as Spirit is fully at work beyond the visible church.

Something else in the Christian witness, while for theologians distinguishable from the Holy Spirit, comes perhaps even closer to what our term *spirit* stands for. We find it in the concept of Christ as the eternal Word. When John speaks of Christ as the Word who was "from the beginning," he identifies him with the creative action of God. "He was in the world, and the world was made through him"—is how John puts it. Surely the action of the spirit of God, when "God began to create," is none other than the action of the Word "through whom also [God] created the world." Again, as John points out, Christ as creative Spirit is the "true light that enlightens every man." It is Christ who, as the true light, endows men and women with the light of knowledge by which they know the physical and psychological worlds. And it is Christ who endows them with the higher knowledge through which they know the ultimate reality sustaining those worlds. Christ as Spirit is both active creative principle and active enlightening principle.

It is when Jesus identified himself with the creative and enlightening action of God, which is to say, with his divine nature, that he could tell his disciples, "Truly, truly, I say to you, before Abraham was, I am." What he said was "I am"—not "I was." He knew that in his divine nature he transcended time past. But he could also say to them, "Lo, I am with you always, to the close of the age." Again what he said was "I am"—not "I shall be." He knew that as the eternal Word he transcended future time. Christ, in his divine nature, is a "timeless Christ" who seems to be very close to the presence we are here referring to as spirit.

It appears that Jesus' timeless nature was not really grasped by his disciples until after his death. But at least Peter and John finally grasped it, as their recorded words attest. Speaking in the temple at Jerusalem some days after Pentecost, Peter referred to him as the "Author of life." In writing of Christ, John declared, "In him was life, and the life was the light of men." To Paul it was clear from the start, because he never encountered Jesus except as timeless Christ. Of this Christ, Paul or one of his followers wrote that "he reflects the glory of God and bears the very stamp of his nature, upholding the universe by his word of power." This same Christ, Paul points out, is "not far from each one of us." He speaks of the mystery of God "hidden for ages and generations but now made manifest to his saints." This mystery, he says, is "Christ in you."

Christ as the Word that was from the beginning is not only the creator and sustainer of the material universe, but the source and basis of the knowing self as well. Working ceaselessly within us and around us, he is not only *being* and *life* to provide the basis for experience, but *light* to allow us to grasp whatever experience the environment offers. What is more, as John points out, the light of understanding cannot be differentiated from the life in human beings. We must take care in discussing him not to allow certain statements about Christ to make us see spirit as something *outside* us. To convey their experiences, the Apostles were obliged, like Jesus himself, to make use of symbols that, if taken only at face value, can lead the mind astray.

Using Christian terms, and keeping this warning in mind, one might make a provisional suggestion about the timeless Christ understood as spirit: it is this Christ that enlightens for us the physical world symbolized by the uninterrupted hydrogen explosion of the sun and the psychological world symbolized by the unknowable but no less energy-releasing life of the human self. This suggestion is perhaps not out of harmony with the faith of certain contemporary Christians that the risen Christ is somehow present to the entire universe. It would be the timeless Christ, too, that makes the "x" behind the total outer environment "become" the tangible physical world, and the "y" behind the total inner environment "become" the knowable psychological world—that is to say, that makes them appear as the realities they are for us. And this being so, it would be the same Christ that, as spirit, effectively joins them for us from moment to moment—whether or not we realized it outside our most intense experiences—into one indivisible but not undifferentiated whole.

This reading of Christ does not pretend to supplant the Christ of traditional theology or of devotional faith. It concerns itself solely with the timeless Christ as immediate presence. In this view, it is Christ as spirit that creates us and sustains us, that gives us light and life. The concept of Christ as creative spirit, which we find in the New Testament, may profitably be used, by those so disposed, as a means of acquainting oneself with the working of spirit.

* * *

My own more recent contact with the Christian witness to spirit came only after a long period of association with Hindu thinking about it. Had I not been prepared by this contact I might not have been open, after taking formal leave of Hinduism, to the intuition of the timeless Christ. During much of that earlier period I had been thinking in terms closely resembling this reading of Christ —as witnessed by the poem "Presence" composed at that time. Curiously enough, it was only after my association with Christianity that I came to see more fully, I think, what Hinduism as I knew it had been saying about spirit. Today I am coming to realize that true religion is a matter of "being and becoming" far more than of belonging or believing however fervent. As a result I feel equally at home in all religions, in a new sense, and I seem to see more clearly what the term spirit is seeking to convey. Because most readers are still unfamiliar with Hindu thinking, I shall examine briefly some of its basic ideas about God, or ultimate reality, before considering their application to spirit.

In the previous chapter we took note of basic doctrines of the Hindu school of Advaita, or strict Nondualism, in relation to the human soul. As we saw there, its conception of the soul grew out of the mystical experiences of certain Vedic sages. These experiences were recorded in scriptural treatises known as Upanishads, most likely between 600 and 200 B.C. Some of the sages claimed to have achieved communion with a reality, Atman, undergirding and giving identity to the individual soul. But there were others who claimed to have communed, in their meditations on the cause of the universe, with a reality undergirding and conferring existence on the physical world. This reality they named Brahman, the suprapersonal Godhead. It too, they said, was indivisible, eternal, all-knowing, all-joyous.

Finally, one of the Vedic sages went farther. In deep contemplation, as he claimed, he discovered that these realities were not two. "This Atman is Brahman" was his memorable declaration. The two apparently separate principles were simply two different ways of experiencing one and the same ultimate truth. It was actually on the basis of this final conclusion that Hindu "scholastic philosophers" constructed, many hundreds of years later, coherent theological systems seeking to explain the relationship of God, soul, and universe. We are not concerned here with the subtle distinctions between the systems, but rather with the original concepts of Brahman and Atman, Godhead and Oversoul.

What then is Brahman? According to the Vedic sages, Brahman is absolute *being:* that which confers on all the objects and happenings in the universe whatever being they possess. It is absolute *awareness:* that which confers knowability on all things and reciprocal awareness on all conscious creatures. It is absolute *joy:* that which affirms the goodness and positive worth of all living and nonliving things and prompts our love of them or satisfaction in them. It is thus called Being-Awareness-Joy Absolute, or Sat-chit-ananda.

The early Vedic sages knew that no description was possible of That which they had found in mystical ecstasy to be not different from themselves. In one of the most ancient of the scriptural

treatises we find the words of a famous Vedic sage: "Now, therefore, the description of Brahman: 'It is not this, not this.' " It is
that, the sage declared, from which speech and mind turn back,
baffled: "Through what should one know That owing to which all
this is known—through what . . . should one know the Knower?"
Brahman looked on in this way, as essentially unknowable, is
known as "Brahman without attributes." And yet in mystical
experience that same Brahman is intuitively known as a positive
something. Balancing the negative description in the previous
examples is this statement of the same sage: "Now the designation of Brahman: 'The truth of truth.' "

The Bhagavad Gita, a scripture composed about 200 B.C., not
only quotes from the Vedic sages but derives many of its teachings from theirs. Recognizing both the real existence of Brahman
and its indescribability, it bears witness to both these aspects:

> It shines through the functions of all the senses
> and yet it is devoid of senses.
> It is unattached, and yet it sustains all.
> It is devoid of qualities, and yet it enjoys them.
> It is without and within all beings.
> It is unmoving and also moving.
> It is incomprehensible because it is subtle.
> It is far away, and yet it is near.
> It is indivisible, and yet it is, as it were, divided
> among beings.
> That Knowable Brahman is the Sustainer of all beings,
> and also their Devourer and Generator.
> The Light even of lights, it is said to be beyond
> darkness.

The Godhead is here spoken of as at one and the same time the
transcendental Divine Ground and the knowable personal God
or Creator, working as spirit works. This memorable statement
is not a mere speculation: it is based on direct experience. When
a mature mystic returns from communion with the attributeless
Brahman, he experiences the Godhead as none other than the
personal God with attributes.

The outward creation was not the only place where the Vedic sages sought out ultimate reality. As we have seen, they looked for it also within themselves, and discovered it as Atman, or the Oversoul. What is Atman? It is the unchanging (though not static) reality that confers being and awareness and joy on the changing human person. As one of the Upanishadic treatises puts it: "Atman, smaller than the small, greater than the great, is hidden in the hearts of all living creatures." The meaning here is not that the Oversoul as inmost self is actually hidden in the heart. It is rather that the inmost self, the spark of Atman, is to be known as a living presence through *meditation in the purified heart* of the individual seeker. Lest the Oversoul underlying the human soul be imagined to be limited to a specific place, the same treatise adds: "Though sitting still, it travels far; though lying down, it goes everywhere."

The Oversoul is really, like the Godhead, beyond description. A concise statement in the Bhagavad Gita, borrowing from Upanishadic teaching, describes it by saying what it is not: "It is never born, nor does it ever die, nor having once been, does it again cease to be." Passages are plentiful in the same tradition, however, where it is spoken of in a way quite as detailed and positive as the way the Godhead is spoken of elsewhere:

> It is through Atman that one knows form, taste, smell,
>   sound, touch, and carnal pleasures.
> Is there anything that remains unknown to Atman? . . .
> It is through Atman that one perceives all objects
>   in sleep or in the waking state.

As we noted, one of the Vedic sages arrived at the realization that there was no difference between the Godhead and the Oversoul. Moreover, it soon became evident that these two were not only transcendent realities; they were seen also as capable of working through the senses and mind in the everyday world. On this latter point the Bhagavad Gita, going beyond the Upanishadic teachings, contributes a further insight. This scripture contains the words of the Lord Krishna, spoken on the field of battle to his disciple, the warrior Arjuna. Profound as the wisdom of the

Vedic sages undoubtedly is, what Krishna teaches in the Gita is especially relevant for average human beings.

Krishna, both through his words and through a stupendous vision granted to his disciple, affirms that he is one with, and the total embodiment of, Vishnu, all-pervading Sustainer of the universe. Whenever righteousness decays and evil flourishes, he declares, the Lord embodies himself as a human being for the reestablishment of righteousness and the destruction of the wicked. His embodiment is known as the avatar or "descent" of Vishnu. The all-pervading reality makes itself available to men in a knowable, immanent form in the human person of the avatar.

Speaking to the disciple, who may be taken as a symbol of each man or woman, Krishna says:

> He who sees me everywhere and sees everything in me,
>   to him I am never lost, nor is he ever lost to me.
> He who, having been established in oneness, worships me
>   dwelling in all beings—
> That yogi, in whatever way he leads his life, lives
>   in me.
> Him I hold to be the supreme yogi, O Arjuna, who looks on
>   the pleasure and pain of all beings as he looks on them
>   in himself.

In Krishna, this passage says, all beings participate. One who *knowingly* participates not only is established in reality but inevitably shows fellow-feeling, compassion, and love to all other creatures. But Krishna is not to be seen as simply one with the personal God; declaring himself to be the "Abode of Brahman," he affirms that he includes the suprapersonal Godhead. In a passage perhaps unique in scripture, he spells out his nature quite clearly:

> Earth, water, fire, air, ether, mind, reason, and ego:
>   such is the eightfold division of my Nature.
> This is my lower nature. But, different from it, know,
>   O mighty Arjuna, my higher nature—
> The Indwelling Spirit by which the universe is sustained.

Know that these two form the womb of all beings:
I am the origin of the entire universe and also its
    dissolution.
There exists nothing whatever higher than I am, O Arjuna.
All is strung on me as a row of gems on a thread. . . .

Know me, O Arjuna, to be the Eternal Seed of all things
    that exist.

Krishna reveals himself as the creative and sustaining Spirit,
the very being of all material things, the life and light of understanding of whatever lives. Working tirelessly in the material
universe and in the inner world of the human soul, though not
contained by them, he assures the indivisible unity of the world.
What we human beings, in our best moments, intuitively sense
as spirit, weaving the world of the sun and the world of the self
into a seamless unity, appears to work in very much the same way
as the timeless Krishna revealed in the Bhagavad Gita.

This reading of him does not pretend to supplant the traditional Hindu devotional or nondualist concepts of Krishna. It concerns itself solely with Krishna as immediate presence. The
concept of him as creative spirit that we find in the Gita may also
be profitably used, by those so disposed, as a means of acquainting themselves with the working of spirit.

* * *

The witness of Christian and Hindu mystics undoubtedly helps
us refine and intensify our sense of spirit's presence—granted
that we already possess a lively belief in spirit. Equally helpful
should be the witness of mystics in many other spiritual traditions. But what if we possess no such lively belief? Can such
witness be of use to someone without some initial amount of
faith? What we must understand is that faith is not the only means
to experience the presence of spirit. Faith itself, without some
personal experience to back it up, is at best hardly more than a
compelling habit of thought. Lack of such faith need not be a
grave obstacle to eventual awareness of spirit.

As suggested in the prologue, through attentiveness to the sun
and to the self it is possible to prepare oneself for becoming open

to the sense of spirit's creative working. I myself have observed stirrings of such a sense whenever I have turned my mind to these two symbols of our total environment. In my own case, the fact that I had already experienced a sense of spirit's presence, seemingly unprepared, made a recurrence easier. I must also point out that I was by no means unfamiliar with the spiritual witness of many religious mystics and also felt I possessed an amount of faith in spirit. Yet those who have not enjoyed such an experience, and who consider themselves to be without faith in spirit, can indeed encourage personal experience through familiarity with the witness of others—provided they also direct their attentiveness to the sun and to the self as present realities.

One thing each of us must remember, believers and unbelievers alike, is that spirit does not depend for its existence on our believing in it. And the fact that we are not always consciously aware of this third and vital aspect of our environment does not mean that we are really out of touch with it. Granted, much of the time we are imperfectly in touch even with the physical world and the psychological world; and we are right in assuming we can never know everything about them, no matter how attentive we are. But our relationship with spirit is of a different order. There is no one of us who is not, even now, in intimate communion with it.

Spirit is not something far removed. Daily, hourly, momently, we come face to face with its working in ourselves and in the world around us. Without its presence we cannot even know the world of the sun or the world of the self. No single one of our sense impressions or mental activities—whether we are fully attentive to it or not—could rise in consciousness without its agency. Spirit is responsible for whatever degree of knowledge of both worlds we possess, and of our own self as well—more than that, for the intuition of their nowness, as of our own. It is what, when from time to time we unconsciously identify ourselves with it in daily life, makes us perceive ourselves as the observer over against both the outer and the inner world.

The conscious experience of spirit, like that of the self, is not something esoteric and mysterious. It is something very simple: so simple that there is nothing simpler. Everything depends on how we approach it. We may try to grapple with spirit through the intellect, as when we analyze objects of everyday experience. When we do so, it appears maddeningly fuzzy or obscure. Even more than the self, it baffles thought, for the very area where it is to be known lies beyond conceptual knowledge (and for that very reason is immediately near). But when we approach it through the kind of intuitive mental activity all of us employ in our moments of most intense absorption, it is not baffling at all. To grasp it then becomes rather a healthy extension of normal awareness.

What is said in the immediately preceding paragraphs is said on the basis of those recurring states of mind already referred to, when it seemed to me that my awareness had reached a new sphere of insight. It was some time after the return to my Western roots that this singular experience began visiting me—a gentle, elusive, state of mind, yet completely convincing and satisfying. Something I can best describe, in its fuller manifestation, as a sense of taking part in the flow of things as they are. My first experience of this state arrived without warning and continued the following day. It seemed as if I had been introduced to a process that was going on all the time but that up till then I had been aware of only for brief moments, if at all.

As a result of this new and longer lasting experience, poems have occurred to me that are more straightforward and simple, far less literary in flavor, than those written and published earlier. A number of them, I believe, convey at least some sense of spirit's presence. On several occasions during the past half-dozen years, while enjoying this state, I have been prompted to write series of loosely related poems. Here are excerpts from one such series along with a few of the single poems.

A NEW-OLD MUSIC

1

It all seemed a strange language
Till I newly understood—
Like the first time a child

Fathoms what a group of grownups
Is openly talking about.

Yet there was really no moment
of revealing . . .
The fact was simply there,
Placidly going on
As it always had been.

2

The crickets have been strumming
Their nightlong
Never ceasing African song:
How comfortable a background
For this new-old music
That holds me . . .

I listen—not, as in childhood,
Because it draws the restive mind away,
But because it is the one song
To listen to, now, here,
When all there is to do
In the summer night
Is to be and to listen.

5

Something has started
Not happening here:
But it started so long ago
That it is hard to say
It ever started not happening at all . . .

6

. . . What it really wants
Is that you just sit and listen
To the very soft, very intricate
New rock and old jazz on the radio,
And that when you rise from your chair

To walk into the next room,
You stop thinking about that music
And start thinking about something fresh,

And keep on being the one
Where it has started not happening . . .

WHERE YOU ARE

The unique advantage of seeing
From this particular
Observation point
Is that you can have your cake
And eat it too

Because sitting here
And looking in or out
You can savor
All the old intensities
Just as they always had been

Even the anguish or anxiety
Or uncertainty
Is yours for the asking
As if you were reading
A favorite romance
For the third or fourth time

But as soon as things get
Too intense
And you almost forget
Where you are and
Almost give away your balance
You can simply lean back
Across the threshold
Poised safely

Between the abyss of now
And the abyss of here.

IN A MUSIC

I walk in a music
where joy is not joy,
where in my wakened self
I can listen to the flowing stream
of my friend Johannes Brahms'
violin sonata
and the hairs on my forearms
stand on end,
but I do not enter in
to the joy:
I lightly walk through the
night air of these sounds
and thrust after thrust of untold
telling rinses my ears,
but the stresses and the contrasts
and the leaping lights of
piano and violin
wash over my wakened self
that is more than a self,
and I walk at peace
in a music
where joy is not joy.

SAYING IT

Every thing and every person
In the world—
Each rock, stick, pebble, pitcher plant,
Cat, saint, beggar, juvenile delinquent—
Is trying to say it
And is in fact saying it.

But the sun says it
Loudest of all,
Because through this prism of yourself
He lights up the whole
Universe.

Enjoyment of this rich awareness of spirit's working in sense
experience and thought comes inexplicably and without warning.
It has confirmed for me the trustworthiness of those related ideas
received earlier through purely poetic inspiration. Longer lasting
than the quick flashes of inspiration from which most of my
strongest earlier poems have sprung, this later experience is a
state of the whole person. True, the poems that come along with
it convey only the vaguest hint of its content—indeed, to some
they may appear to speak less authoritatively than the earlier
poems born of an inspiration unaccompanied by the sense of
spirit's presence. Nevertheless its compelling though quite un-
dramatic revelation is truly a "pearl of great price." Whatever the
value of the poems it produces, the state of mind itself—in its
influence on character as well as its psychological content—bears
the stamp of authenticity.

Obviously the experience I refer to applies to more than surface sense experience and surface mental processes. At the same
time, its very occurrence, and recurrence, shows me that the
meaning of both one's sense experience and one's thought *can*
be enhanced. Many of us have observed the egoless attentiveness
that comes to the consciously working and dedicated craftsman
or artist or teacher or scholar or priest, often after long practice.
The very same result is to be observed in the awareness I am
discussing: here, too, we obtain a deeper insight into what is
given us through the senses and translated for us by the mind.
That attentiveness, the fruit of a truly healthy exercise of the
senses, is a fit celebration of the basic elements of everyday life—
what certain ancient Hindu sages saw as the elements of ether
(space), air, fire, water, and earth. Once it has been attained, we
need write poems for no reason other than pure delight. Our
daily life has become our best poem.

In discussing such an experience one must try to be scrupulously honest, so as not to mislead. I must remind readers that what I report and what conclusions I draw are not based on a continuous flow of heightened awareness. My personal familiarity with what we are here calling spirit is based solely on these repeated but discontinuous experiences of mine. When not enjoying direct awareness, however, memory of it emboldens an unswerving faith in its credibility and the possibility of its undeserved return. During such times of dryness (which constitute, so far, most of one's life) I make no effort to glance directly at spirit as I suggest we do at the sun. My approach is more like what we have to use with the self—an approach through indirection.

In dealing with spirit, we have to keep our thinking as rigorously simple as we can. If we have no memory of its presence to strengthen faith, we prepare ourselves best for enjoying direct awareness of its creative working by thinking *around* it, making use of its descriptions by others (where they appear to be based on personal experience) and of its evident manifestations on all sides. As already noted, merely thinking *about* spirit, as if it were an object of sight or thought, is liable to wall us away further from the direct experience of it available to us, wherever we are ready, every moment of our lives.

* * *

We come then finally to another question: How are we to recognize spirit's working as we come face to face with it in everyday life? While we still think of our environment in terms of its three aspects, spirit appears to us to function on its own in the world of the sun and the world of the self. Until now we have looked on these worlds as stemming primarily from the sun and the self: that was why we chose these two as the symbols through which to acquaint ourselves with them. But as we grow more receptive to spirit, we see it rather as working *through* the sun and the self, and their worlds, than as independent of them. Gradually we come to see everything as a witnessing to spirit.

Spirit is at work, of course, on unperceived levels as well as on the observable, everyday one. In the world of the sun, the finer workings of spirit take a myriad unperceived forms. Oxidation and similar chemical reactions, photosynthesis, crystallization, osmosis, biological evolution of species, reproductive functions, cloning, and the like all bear witness to it. And on a subtler level, atmospheric vibrations, light waves, atomic and molecular activity, positive and negative electricity, gravity, and the rest. In the world of the self, its finer workings are found in sense impressions, the mechanisms that trigger intellectual and emotional reaction to those impressions, ego-identification, will power, the sexual impulse, as well as in the urge to repress or release unconscious drives, the response mechanisms of joy and love (and dislike), artistic inspiration, extrasensory perception, intuition, and a host of others—all based on nerve cell activity in the brain.

These unperceived phenomena in both worlds are observed chiefly through the intellect. Physical scientists investigate those in the world of the sun, but only such as are to be observed outside themselves. Psychologists and psychoanalysts can study those in the world of the self, even within themselves. But few of us are in a position to be attentive to any of them or to develop a feeling of at-homeness with them, or even to corroborate them. And few if any of us have any need to.

Whether in the world of the sun or the world of the self, the observable level is where most of us find our best opportunity to familiarize ourselves with spirit's working. That is where it is continuously revealed. The area of immediate experience is the one area where all of us—the most creative or scientifically disciplined as well as the least gifted of us—touch the working of spirit directly. It is through observing what spirit *does openly* rather than through drawing inferences about its working or studying what is said about it that we learn gradually to grasp it by intuition. Never forgetting, as we do so, that full awareness of its presence is possible only when we are fully ready and the time has come.

For a foretaste of what manifests itself spontaneously once the time has actually come and we enjoy a conscious attentiveness to the world of the sun in the light of spirit, we have not far to seek. Provided we have somewhat clarified our attentiveness to sense objects by regularly practiced attentiveness to the sun, we can readily note the working of spirit in the gifts of hearing, touch, taste, sight, and smell. Each moment after we awake in the morning, they bear witness to it throughout the day. As we wash and dress, as we eat our meals, as we carry out our household or office duties, as we read the newspaper or listen to the radio or watch television, as we deal with our family, as we entertain guests, as we prepare for sleep at night—it is the same. Or again, while we come in contact with the natural outdoor world, or lose ourselves in the bustle of city life, or travel in foreign lands, or throw ourselves into sports or other sorts of outgoing relaxation.

There is not a moment of our waking life in any of these and a thousand other circumstances when the five senses are not busy offering us their gifts, through the grace of spirit. None of us, while we still have to will our attention to that fact consciously, can recognize spirit's working in them continuously. But provided we faithfully cultivate attentiveness to the objects of the senses through regularly practiced attentiveness to the sun, awareness of its presence grows ever more frequent. Finally we reach a state where recognition of spirit's working is spontaneous and effortless.

When we have achieved the necessary centeredness of attention to savor the working of spirit in the gifts of the senses while they are being given, we can then begin to look effectively within. Through regularly practiced attentiveness to the self, we touch the working of spirit as well in the surface reactions that sense objects evoke in our minds—in our feelings and thoughts and desires and purposes. We may even come, eventually, to differentiate between the immediate sense impressions and our reaction to them.

After we have thus begun to clarify our attentiveness to the surface phenomena of the inner world, we learn to recognize the working of spirit not only in our reactions to the objects of sense in the world outside us and in our physical body, but in the innumerable related activities they give rise to in the mind. We begin to be more alertly aware of those two aspects in spirit's inner working already briefly touched on: the function that bestows *being* and *life* on the objects of the inner world, and the function (always accompanying it) that sheds the *light* of understanding on those objects and on that light itself.

We can look within ourselves and see the working of spirit, for example, in the emotions roused in us by music or poetry or painting. We can see it in various other reactions on our part to what is going on around us: in our honest admiration of some other person (whether for heroism or self-sacrifice or endurance, for industry, for integrity), in healthy-minded hope or ambition, in responsible political concern, in unchauvinistic patriotism, and so on. And equally in the enthusiasms sparked by watching various types of dance or sport. (One may tend to think of spirit only in connection with the more lofty or serious pursuits—with churchgoing or private devotions or profound study or service of humanity. But that is to set limits to the illimitable.) We can see spirit at work in innumerable other forms of emotion: without its presence and cooperation they could not be, could not achieve actuality in the inner space of the world of the self.

Even the caricatures of such emotions—shallow aestheticism, undiscriminating hero worship, obsessive attachment or anticipation, violent political or sports partisanship, blind jingoism, and the like—derive whatever power they possess, positive or negative, from spirit's mysterious presence and activity. Creative spirit, for its own hidden purposes, as it were, allows the existence of the negative and the evil—perhaps as much for a spur to the positive and the good as for a contrast to set these off to advantage and give them meaning. Moreover, we should recognize that in anyone who consciously and sincerely seeks awareness of the working of spirit, distorted emotions leading to negative manifestations such as these can hardly arise, or, if they do arise, cannot long persist.

In the several stages of love, it is the same as with other emotions. We find the working of spirit in childish self-love, in love of friend, of wife or husband or other seriously chosen sex partner, of children (one's own or others'), and finally in love of humanity. And, too, in love's misapplication: emotional parasitism, possessiveness, lustfulness, and so on. Through positive loves, seen as the working of spirit, we slowly rise beyond the demands of the ego-self. Through distorted forms of love we learn by suffering, if we are lucky, that true peace of mind and true joy cannot be found where there is identification with ego.

In our casual everyday exercise of the mental faculties of analysis and discrimination and logical reasoning, or in intensive study, or in scholarly or scientific research, or in the subtleties of philosophical or theological conjecture, we likewise touch the working of spirit. Here, as before, we observe two aspects of its working: the aspect that bestows being and life, and the aspect that sheds the light not only of thought activity but of awareness of the being and life of the light itself.

We are especially closely in touch with spirit in the experience of wonder and worship and prayer (including mystical contemplation). We note a difference, though, between these and the other evidences of the working of spirit we have been looking at. We should not, in this instance, try to be alert to them while we are experiencing them. Their nature, being intuitive, is such that they cannot persist (as many other workings of spirit can) when one sets oneself apart from them. As with any complete participation in sense experience or feeling experience or thought experience, there is no opportunity to be self-conscious about them. Yet we can learn to appreciate what they mean for us, and be grateful for them, *after* they have passed. And to realize that without their occasional recurrence we should lose an intimate contact with spirit and our life would be poorer and shallower—and less human.

Through looking back in this way on moods of wonder and worship and prayer or meditation in terms of spirit, we can see, in time, all manifestations of spirituality everywhere as workings of one creative energy. Seeing them in truer perspective, we can look on their manifold forms in the various religions without prejudgment, and finally with generous acceptance, no matter what sweeping claims may sometimes be put forward for them by dedicated believers in those religions (or indeed in our own). We shall then see them all in terms of their positive content. We shall recognize them, whether or not they appeal to us personally, as valid ways of enabling men and women of differing temperaments and cultures to approach nearer to a realization of spirit itself.

* * *

There are all manner of instances where the world of the senses and the mind are even more closely intertwined. Here, too, we can learn to observe the working of spirit and so increase our at-homeness with it and intensify our faith in it. It is manifest, for example, in our willed performance of daily duty. Destiny may have chosen us to be a conscientious parent, or a generous-hearted instructor, or a responsible businessman or politician or judge, or a dedicated scientist, or a vigorous manual worker, or a specialist in any one of a multitude of other occupations. If we have been regularly attentive to the sun and to the self, we can recognize the working of spirit not only in the actual sense impressions involved in our performance of duty, but in the interpersonal relationships we are led into, with their burdens of obligation, interest, care, patience, and so on.

In any successful encounter with another person the presence of spirit is, even if usually overlooked, immediate and compelling. In every such encounter except the most trivial or calculating—in encounters with animals and birds and other living creatures, as well as with humans—attention is focused solely on what is now and here. Such encounters are one of our closest approaches to the experience of Now, and indeed often exhibit perfect, though fleeting, examples of it. In approaching our personal relationships in terms of spirit, the whole fabric of our social life is obviously enriched. And once we have learned to savor these relationships without distraction, *while we are enjoying them,* we can, if we look deeper, touch the working of spirit also in the various feelings and thoughts and intuitions they arouse, and at last in the awareness that illumines them and us.

Beyond such personal contacts, the working of spirit can become evident to us in the social structure itself: in the great ideals of democracy and our response to them, in the best goals of Marxist socialism if we happen to live in a Marxist country (whose professed goal is expressed in the well-known maxim: "From each according to his abilities, to each according to his needs"), in the good in every form of society. Its working is also somehow in evidence—at a lower level of intensity, and with less of clarity—in the frequent betrayals or abrogations of those ideals.

In society we shall recognize spirit at work wherever men and women alert others to the dangers of environmental pollution and the all-importance of observing the laws of ecology. Wherever they defend the rights of the consumer against unreasonable exploitation by producers. Wherever they work unsensationally to show men the uselessness of aggressive wars. Wherever they combat poverty and the wrongs of racism, of religious animosity, of prejudice in every form. And equally in our own responses to their efforts. As before, we shall also meet it in the responses of those who oppose and combat them. There is indeed no place where spirit is idle (as Krishna indicates in the Bhagavad Gita), though we touch it closest in what is positive and constructive.

It is not in the nature of human society, and probably never will be, to offer a perfect revelation of spirit (that is, except where the individual observer is already open to it). But from the point of view we are seeing things from, the most nearly ideal society would be one where men and women who desired it were offered the best chance to cultivate openness to the mystery of spirit's working—as it is to be known in itself and through attentiveness to the sun and to the self—and thus the best chance to claim their birthright as humans.

One central fact about spirit remains to be considered. It is spirit, as we have seen, that weaves into one living whole the world of the sun (the world of sense perception) and the inner perceiver or self in our best moments. So too it is spirit that, when we confine ourselves to the world within, weaves the world of the self and the inner perceiver into one. The self quite obviously is the subject or inner perceiver in relation to its own world as well as to the world of the sun. In both cases we may think of it as a conduit through which creative spirit enters the world—whether the physical world or the psychological world. As we concluded earlier on the basis of self-examination, the self can be positively known in the intuitive awareness "I am," "I am aware," and "I love" (in their most rigorous sense). If then the self is seen as a conduit for spirit, it would appear that this threefold intuitive awareness is *spirit itself*. That being so, it may occur to some readers to ask to whom the positive awareness "I do" or "I want" or "I will" or "I think" or "I say" applies. Is it to spirit, too? Such awareness, I submit, also involves spirit—but at one remove, so to speak.

When we looked at the Christian and Hindu concepts of the person or soul, we found that in both instances human beings were thought to possess free will. That should mean that the person or soul is self-activating. At the same time, saints and mystics have stated over and over again that everything is done "by God's will"—which would seem to mean that men and women (and other creatures) only *appear* to act freely. Who is it that does everything? Saint Paul affirms not only that through Christ "all things were created," but, referring to himself, that "it is no longer I who live, but Christ who lives in me." If we take the word "Christ" here to be equivalent to spirit, it would appear that the real doer of every action, the real desirer, the real willer, the real thinker, the real speaker, is spirit itself.

This thought may seem to challenge the meaning—indeed, threaten the validity—of everything we do or feel or think or the like. But it is not so. Spirit does indeed impel all living creatures to action and feeling and thought. But so long as we have not differentiated the self from the ego *in experience,* the thought "I do" or "I want" or "I will" or "I think" or "I say" continues to rise with each action we perform, each purpose we implement, each desire we cherish, each thought we entertain, each word we utter. When we finally participate in spirit, when we have become continuously aware of its presence and creative working, we then act and feel and think and speak *as spirit.* We become instruments of spirit. But until we directly see the distinction between self and ego, spirit itself weaves the sense of independent ego into all these activities.

Thus the idea of free will is a true idea for us, and we cannot refuse responsibility for our deeds, good or bad, saying that it is not we but the spirit that is to blame. Few would deny that the threefold diagram of our environment as made up of the world of the sun, the world of the self, and the world of spirit must be treated as accurate and real and be made use of so long as we have not yet realized the presence of spirit. So too, the notion of the individual ego (the ego-self) as doer or the like must be held to be accurate and real and be made use of until such a time. It is when we have intellectually accepted the idea of spirit as doer or the like, without making an effort to realize it in experience, that danger of misinterpretation arises.

The concept of free will and self-determination is no more than a provisional explanation to fit present disability. If we know that, we can look forward to a time when we shall see our diagram of three worlds, and this concept itself, as equally the working of spirit. Once that time has come, we shall have become conscious instruments of spirit. But knowing it is vital only to ourselves, for spirit is at work everywhere and in everything we accomplish— even our failures and mistakes.

This sampling of activities of spirit in the surface worlds of sun and self is far from exhaustive. I have called attention to some notable examples to suggest the numberless areas where we can observe them and see them for what they are—once we begin to feel a real need to do so. By being attentive to them, we open ourselves further to eventual intuitive awareness of what we may call the Now of spirit. Meanwhile we intensify our *faith* in spirit's immediate presence. That faith assures us we shall apprehend it one day, in complete relaxation, as the all-pervasive vitalizing and illuminating principle within the human environment, the two worlds of sun and self—and as the immediate presence in the awareness of its own power of illumining: the "Light even of lights."

* * *

If the sun and the self are vital to the physical and psychological worlds, spirit is even more profoundly vital to their being and survival. The sun and the self may be said in a certain sense to *be* the worlds they stand for. They are the continuing physical and psychological causes of those worlds. Without them the physical world and the psychological world could neither have come into existence nor have gone on evolving. But spirit may be said to be related to its world (the total environment comprising the Now of the sun and the Now of the self) in a more profound sense. It is not the physical or the psychological cause of that world in the sense of having directly provided the matter or energy of which it is made up. But it is, if I may use the phrase, that world's existential cause. It is its very being and light.

A reference to Christian cosmology may help clarify for some readers this admittedly difficult idea. When God began to create —as the profoundly intuitive Hebrew creation myth has it—the spirit of God "was moving over the face of the waters," the unknowable "x" or matrix of the universe, and out of that moving the two worlds were born: first the objective world and at last the subjective. Both the Christian and the Hindu witness affirm that creative spirit not only gives being-and-life to the one and being-and-light to the other, but *is* being and life and light. These three are what bestow for us the dimension of actuality upon a too often abstract, intellectually conceived, three-dimensional world of matter and mind. Without spirit, there can be no actuality. For among the basic creative workings of spirit must be accounted time itself—which provides the fourth dimension of existential reality for both matter and mind, and in which being-and-life reveals itself as becoming. It is only through time that the chain of what we know as "cause and effect" can exist and operate. Again, paradoxically, it is only in direct experience of Now that time is annulled, that is to say, resolved into its source.

I myself no longer favor thinking in terms of religious or mythological or philosophical concepts except as they help to intensify my nonabstract experiential contact with actuality. Yet for those who know how to relate statements of scripture to everyday experience, the Hebrew creation myth brings home how intimately spirit is involved in every level of our environment, outer and inner. After all, most people can usually make conscious contact with spirit only through intuitive concepts. For them, some sort of mythology is necessary if they are to be able to think about it and exchange ideas about it. Only a very few can see spirit in its naked essence—apart from all representation, either personal or ideational—as being implicit in the law of becoming and at the same time not separate from either objects or events.

While we are still forced to think about our situation in terms of the two contrasting worlds of sun and self, joined into one by spirit, we may understandably conceive of spirit—as in the poem "Presence" at the start of this chapter—as somehow existing between them. Once we have learned through attentiveness to sun and self to enjoy their worlds instead by participation, we recognize the division as mere makeshift—an invention, imprecise though necessary, of intellect. For there is actually no meeting point between them for spirit to exist in and work in.

SEAMLESS ROBE

Dare I divide
Except in thought
My watchful stuff
From the spread face
Of the world's
Wide wovenness?
What old deceit
Is this, that says
The jointed grass
That cloaks my hill,
Swaying its buff
Upstanding grace
To the small wind's
Insistencies,
Bends to another
Force than I,
And infirm man's
Distracted lot
Somehow walls
Itself about—
Holding his headlong
Impulses
Not of a piece
With earthliness?

Such is the empty
Boast of thought,
Oblivious of its
Destined part,
Self-wrapt from being's
Quenchless source,
Tricked by some
Unsaid design
Into thin ways
To shut it from
The total sphere

That girds it round,
Joining its own
And earthy ways
In an unbroken
Warp and woof.
See, all about,
In wind and grass,
Earth's urgings and
Long purposes:
All in steadfast
Rhythm incline
To the same pulse
That beats in mine.

One cannot say precisely where the outer world ends and the inner world begins, or where the inner world ends and the outer world begins. They are not only interrelated but interpenetrating. As energy, the outer physical world penetrates to its farthest depths the inner psychological world, and as interpretive reaction and conception the inner psychological world of the individual penetrates to its farthest reaches his or her outer physical world. Spirit, which for convenience the intellect conceived as existing and working between them, is everywhere.

In turning our attention to the all-importance of spirit, I do not mean to negate in any way the importance or indeed necessity of the physical and psychological worlds in themselves. As we shall see one day for ourselves, if we are lucky, once we have realized spirit as a very present and living reality our gratitude for both worlds will be deepened and our participation in them enriched. We shall see them as indispensable partners in its working with us and in us and for us.

This chapter has sought to intensify our attentiveness to spirit and its working by treating it, in the main, *as if* it were separate. Our very use of this makeshift is our admission that we are not yet fully open to its immediate presence. Yet this is the only way most of us can at last learn to participate in spirit intuitively as inseparable from the other two aspects of our environment. The next chapter tries to evolve a working method, for those readers who have become better acquainted and more at home than before with all three worlds, to put into daily practice what we have learned. The method may not be an infallible guide toward the now-and-here experience in which we see things as they truly are. But I trust that for most serious persons who seek such a goal but have had little or no fruitful contact with traditional religion it will open a way. Since I myself have been experimenting in this direction, I have enjoyed more frequent and convincing intuitions than ever before of the presence of creatively working spirit.

✶ THE ROAD TO NOW

INTENTIONS

To walk expertly
Through time and air,
Not forcing and not
Yielding, aware
Always of the rich
Stillness you bring
With you from beyond
Duration and
Changing atmosphere.

To love and be
Loved as the new hour
Allows; to sing
If singing inspires
Fidelity
To what your end is
And what you are.

And so pass surely
Through time and air,
Intent upon your
Intrinsic way,
Alert and wholly
Committed here
To what arrivings
Define this day.

T he Road to Now is the road leading to experience of every-day life in terms of the living moment. It is in no way a hidden or secret road: there is no question of anyone's having to search for it. It already lies open to everyone. In a certain sense, setting out on it is not even a matter of our own choosing. Whether we know it or not, we actually set foot on this road the moment we first draw breath, and we continue along it until death. Yet despite all this it can be an elusive, even a devious, road. What makes all the difference is whether we travel it un-knowingly or knowingly—whether we do more than stumble along it blindly, trusting time and good luck to bring us to our journey's end. To set foot knowingly on the road means to start the process by which we finally come to terms with each object or event in its immediacy.

We are now ready to set out on the road in that sense. In the preceding chapters we have made ourselves at home with the Now of the sun and the Now of the self, and to a degree with the Now of spirit. The familiarity we have gained is largely an intel-lectual familiarity. Possessed of it, we are prepared to consider and begin practicing a few exercises to become more intuitively open to the working of spirit, the "crux of now," in daily life. It is not enough to think about these matters. To zero in on present actuality we must create the conditions for knowing the world of the sun and the world of the self as made one in spirit, now and here.

First we shall take up a few simple exercises having to do with the sun (as symbol and source of the physical world), and then a few having to do with the self (as symbol and source of the psychological world). After considering these, we shall see how we may bring the Now of spirit into the scheme. Even a partly successful attentiveness to the first two elements of our environ-ment—whether taken separately or together—should result in an increased natural openness to the third, which is really insepara-ble from the other two except in abstract thought. No one leading a busy life in the everyday world can practice all the exercises. Each reader may choose whichever of them seems appropriate.

* * *

Before taking up actual exercises for learning to be attentive to the sun, and through it to the world it symbolizes, let us remind ourselves once more of its meaning for us personally. What is immediately impressive about the sun is the twofold fact stressed in the first chapter: through its original positioning the sun brought our physical environment into being, and through its continuing presence and activity during billions of years, it has made possible the development of our physical bodies and the eventual manifesting of our conscious persons.

Our own biological evolution, extending through unimaginably long periods of time, is based of course on a material evolution of far longer duration. It is, as we now believe, the result of a process of natural selection that allowed those mutant forms to survive that were best adapted to their environment, and produced in its unfolding a balance between living and nonliving forms. Evolution on the inorganic, organic, and psychic levels is responsible for sensitivity in plants, sense experience and elementary consciousness in animals and other nonhuman creatures, and a unique self-awareness in combination with sensation, feeling, and thought in humans. As we have noted, without the sun's original positioning and its continuing presence, none of this could have been or could now be. For this reason alone the sun deserves our recognition and gratitude—even our awe. Not to be ignored, as well, is the fact that from the central sun itself have come those containing layers of gas without which we could not have survived the consuming flow of its potent rays. Indeed, according to the theory we have provisionally accepted, almost all the matter that makes up the earth and all the material objects and creatures upon it were once associated with the incipient sun.

Another fact is equally impressive. Like a self-effacing teacher, the sun, having brought forth and intensified our capacity to know, has thereby revealed to us not only itself but a cosmos of matter and energy *beyond* itself, of which it is literally an infinitesimal part—a cosmos that, in its turn, is responsible for the sun's own development and continuing presence. Indeed, it is through the evolution of the consciousness and self-awareness fathered by the sun that the cosmos is able, so to speak, to "know itself." It would almost appear, as the Hindu mystic Vivekananda has suggested, that intelligence is somehow "involved" in physical matter itself and must inevitably emerge when the conditions are right. Again, by the emergence of the capacity for logical reasoning, the cosmos is enabled (through human agency) to recreate in a new way the primal phenomenon, fusion of hydrogen-atom nuclei, by which our solar system—and conceivably other solar systems and even the material universe as a whole—has been deployed in space.

Beyond this, through the same process of evolution, we humans have been gifted with the sense of a reality transcending everything else the sun has revealed to us, and yet at the same time immanent in all. By allowing our psychological evolution, it has made it possible for a few humans to arrive at direct mystical intuition of spirit as manifested through both the world of matter and the world of thought-energy. It has allowed them to come at both the self that knows the physical and psychological worlds, and the transcendent creative principle behind both these worlds and the knowing self. This does not suggest that the sun is the *source* of the creative principle. But it does mean that it was only through the sun's grace, as it were, that we could evolve to the point where we could conceive that that reality exists.

At the beginning of our practice, before such thinking becomes second nature, we may find it useful to remind ourselves of these ideas each day. Later we may need only to refer to them briefly when we find we have momentarily neglected them.

The central practice will be to accustom the mind to experiencing the sun, and later each physical object we encounter, as a *present fact*. To train the mind to know the sun in this way, we may make it a habit to greet it at three or four crucial points of the day: first, if possible, when it appears on the eastern horizon, or at least when we have our earliest chance to see it; second, at midday, when it is directly overhead; third, at sundown, as it approaches the western horizon; and fourth, if we are awake, at or near midnight, when we have turned to a position roughly opposite it and so can greet it only in imagination.

When the sun rises, we may greet it with wonder and even (if we are temperamentally fitted) with love, looking at it directly but guardedly so as not to cause injury to the eyes. We may try to think not that it is "there" and we are "here," but that since it is unmoving in relation to the earth, its location is perpetually "here." As material cause of almost everything material in us and our world, and as energy-pulsing source of our very thinking processes and our continuing existence, its presence may be held to be true center. We, as its effects and dependents, are physically *not* center (any more than we are always standing with our head "up") but are turning with our portion of the earth toward a point where we can say that physically both we and the sun are here and that we are indeed "standing up." (To help us visualize this fact, we may imagine as we watch the rising sun the earth's turning *toward* it until the sun stands directly above us, and then imagine it turning back again to where we are.)

With the ancient Egyptians and the contemporary Hopis and other Pueblo tribes, we may also feel grateful for what we and humanity and all living beings owe to the sun: simply everything immediately real to us (including our knowledge of the visible universe *outside* our solar system). Grateful, too, for its promise of a new day.

On a cloudy morning the task is far less easy than when the sky is clear. If one cannot see the sun's orb as it first appears in the east, the mind may also be clouded. It may revert to the same forgetfulness that allows so many of us to put the sun out of our attention, habitually, even when we could look at it. When we cannot see its first triumphant rays, a mental effort is demanded to think of the promise of the rising sun. The effort, though hard, is not impossible. On such mornings we may repeat mentally or aloud some text having to do with the sun. Sometimes an ancient scriptural passage will not appeal to us. In that case, we may compose something for ourselves or simply think through the thoughts about the sun that we considered just now before taking up these exercises.

A second favorable time for greeting the sun is noon. When its blaze is almost directly overhead is the time we can say, if ever it can be said with anything like precision, "The sun is here, and I am here." It is the one time when our relationship with it is perceived more in terms of fact than of illusion.

If we enjoy an opportunity for sunbathing at noon, we may tell ourselves that after we have been lying in sunlight for 8.3 minutes, we are receiving light waves that have left the sun's surface only 8.3 minutes earlier—as we have been, of course, all the time without thinking about it. While directly exposing our body to it, conscious awareness of the fact may increase our sense of intimacy with the sun. Since to look at the sun is probably harmful for most eyes even at times other than an eclipse, I now look at it either by the edge of an overhanging roof or through the branches of a tree or between my fingers. This is the time for us to realize the awesome presence both of the sun's creative and sustaining power and of its power to destroy.

The immediate source of our life and continued existence on earth has been a source of death for many creatures in the past— during the Ice Age, for instance, when its outflow of energy is thought to have been lessened—and could be so in the future. That it is just 93 million miles from us, which represents close proximity as compared to the 26 trillion miles between us and the nearest living star in our own galaxy, is an astounding fact. A stupendous mass of hydrogen, some 864,000 miles in diameter and 330,000 times as heavy as earth, "burning" at a fantastically high temperature, is slowly turning by fusion of hydrogen-atom nuclei into helium and in the process emitting an unimaginably large flow of radiant energy in all directions. As we noted earlier, this continuous hydrogen explosion is held by astrophysicists to be made possible by layers upon layers of gas that insulate the sun's core. Their density, they tell us, is just sufficient to keep its temperature at the degree needed for the fusion to continue, yet allow enough solar energy to escape so as to permit life on earth. Surely a cause for awe, if not actual terror, as well as wonder.

It is idle and possibly harmful—unless one is an avowed mystic —to let this sort of thinking usurp more than a fraction of one's time. Normal daily life has to be responsibly carried on. Yet it is not unhealthy to steep the mind, for a few minutes at noon, in the nowness, the immediate presence, of the all-powerful sun. And to recognize in it, with as little surface emotion as possible, a showing forth of primal creative power. It is a good time to think, too, of the actual fact of the earth's hanging in the void of space and daily revolving at a speed of slightly more than 1,000 miles an hour, while traveling through space in an elliptical orbit of 365¼ days' duration. And of its placement at such an angle that the days grow longer and the sun (in the Northern Hemisphere) appears earlier and farther north each day from the winter solstice in December to the summer solstice in June. And of its reversing the process during the succeeding half-year.

Because it is so intrinsic a part of our surroundings, we tend to take the sun completely for granted and overlook the miracle that it is. Yet the sun is, as we should recognize by now, the essence of our immediate objective world, and at midday it offers a vision of its actuality so far as we can realize it through our physical eyes and through the information that astrophysicists give us of its makeup. To become familiar with it as a physical reality makes it easier to grasp all physical objects as they are, in the miracle of their immediacy. Dawn and sundown are also excellent times to recall our actual physical relationship to the sun—as is midnight, if we are then awake. At all such times the thought that the sun is always at noon can be highly suggestive and stimulating.

It is almost impossible to overestimate the efficacy of the sight of the naked sun for spurring one to intense recollection of our true situation and to intensified practice of the exercises in this fourth stage of our journey on the Road to Now. I have found that all the subsequent disciplines to be mentioned here become far less forced, far more natural, if I can manage to see this living star at least a few times each day where it burns unchanging in the sky.

Sometimes because of clouds we cannot see the sun's orb as it shines dazzlingly bright at noon. Then, too, the mind inevitably reverts to forgetfulness of the sun—just as it does when it is concealed at dawn. Here again a strong mental effort is required. On such sunless days I use one of my own poems about it as a reminder of the sun's presence and its overwhelming importance to humanity as a source of energy, life, and consciousness.

LEAP OF VISION

Dawn breaks where sundown was,
Sundown fades where dawn will be:

As you ride your tethered earth
Circling through imensities,
If you'd not be hindered by
Time-born clouds of old deceit,
Let vision leap beyond
To the no-where of clear light:

There, with every dancing mote
In truth's all-devouring eye,
You may greet the still Day Star
At high noon suspended free

As he pulses life and thought
With a myriad other suns,
In a nowness fresh and bright
Past all sundowns and all dawns.

A third favorable time to greet the sun is at day's end. As we watch the sun apparently sinking toward the horizon—that is to say, as the rim of the horizon rises toward the magnified disk of the sun and our own position moves farther and farther from it—once more we may try to give it our complete attention. We should not think solely of the beauty or glory it now appears to be surrounded with, but try to feel a gratitude and even love for its presence and for its providential and yet perfectly inevitable functioning. The place where we stand or sit has become a "there" in contrast to the sun's changeless "here." Once again, to help us visualize the fact, we may imagine the earth's turning *toward* the sun until it stands directly above us, as at noon, and then its turning back again to where we now are. At this point we may bid temporary farewell to the sun, the central fact of our physical being, in confident expectation of its return on the morrow.

Now is an appropriate time to think, if one likes, of earth's orbiting around the sun as a sort of circumambulation, like that which pious Christians sometimes make around a holy place of pilgrimage and pious Hindus make around not only sacred places but images of the deity or of saints. For a religiously minded person, it is as if earth is setting humanity an example of uninterrupted reverence. At all times, also, we may recall any of the other facts that astronomers and astrophysicists have taught us about the sun. And should the sun be hidden by clouds, so that there is no splendid sunset, we can make the same sort of mental effort we made before to recall its presence—through repeating a scriptural or poetic text or some reminder we have composed for ourselves.

At midnight if we happen to be awake (or at the time of retiring for sleep) we may try to remember the sun once again. We may think of ourselves not as "here on top" of the earth, with our head and the roof of our house "up," but as hanging "there below" in relation to the sun, which is always at the "here" of noon. Now is the best time to think of ourselves as just about to start on the incredibly long and swift journey (at slightly more than 1,000 miles an hour) back to our starting point at noon.

At all times of day, but now especially, we may try to think intensely of the earth's rotating on its axis as it circles the sun, and of the sun as standing absolutely still in relation to it (and us). We may also picture earth and the other planets around the sun: first, for convenience, as strung out in a long line extending from it, and then as orbiting around it. It is no doubt hard for many people to form such a mental picture. But in this way, just as through the suggested exercises at dawn, noon, and sundown, the mind becomes more resilient. All such exercises, though taxing at first, imperceptibly become easier as time passes, until they are almost effortless.

We have noted that in this world of matter-energy no point of view represents things as they are with absolute precision. And that in order to carry on life at all successfully we have to accept things as they appear on the surface. The exercises in connection with the sun are to be practiced simply with a view to seeing things as precisely as we can. In other words, while we are not expected to *see* the sun as a compact mass of hydrogen atoms turning into helium atoms (the naked eye being unable to perceive its fine structures), we *are* expected to recognize where our observation (as when we judge its position and "movement") is based on optical illusion.

If the exercises prove congenial and to some degree take hold of us, we may occasionally make contact in this way with the sun between the stated times. It cannot be stressed too often that such contacts, however brief, are always a powerful source of spiritual arousal. Meanwhile we shall also be forming the habit of turning our attentiveness, wherever possible, to the multitude of reports of the sense organs about the physical world that the sun makes possible.

There are any number of ways of paying attention to the details of our immediate sense world—whether taken as part of a general situation or taken in themselves without relation to anything else. They include such trivialities as observing, in the city, the sort of shoes (even shoelaces or other accessories) a passerby on the street is wearing, or, during a walk in the country, picking up a green walnut from the ground and bruising the skin so as to concentrate on its pungent sweet scent, or listening to the talking of a brook as it courses over its stones. Or similarly, being aware of the tightness or looseness of our own clothes, or being attentive to the sensation of the body as a whole, or any of a thousand other seemingly unimportant yet all equally immediate details.

Such exercises, casual or deliberate, may best be left to our own ingenuity. None of them should interfere with our properly carrying out our daily duties. But there are frequent occasions during any day—especially when we are relaxing or at meals, but even in the intervals between specific activities demanding our whole attention—when it is possible to direct attention toward what we are experiencing through the senses.

Just as attentiveness to the sun stimulates a more attentive awareness of sense objects, so attentiveness to sense objects stimulates a more attentive awareness of the sun. At last, by gradual degrees, we should become more continuously (though not prepossessingly) aware of the sun in the stillness of its Now. The result, again, should be a much richer identification not only with all the material objects around us as we encounter them, but with all the living creatures we come in contact with or think about.

Some of the practices I have outlined can best be carried out, certainly, if we live in the country. Still, if our interest is intense we can pursue them in the midst of a bustling, crowded city as well. The exercises centered around the sun itself may be practiced in a city park or on top of a building or (more taxing) in imagination, instead of in an open field or on a hill or in a garden. But the occasional sight of the sun is indispensable. Those exercises centering around attentiveness to the reports of the five senses may be practiced at any time or place.

It would be idle to pretend that every one of us is in a position to practice these or any such exercises in our present circumstances. Even granting that we are possessed of the indispensable sufficient desire to know things as they are, clearly a certain amount of leisure time is needed to work up confidence in the efficacy of such a program, let alone undertake to carry it out. A first aim for many persons with a sufficient desire but scant opportunity is somehow to earn such leisure time. No one should underestimate the obstacle that everyday preoccupations pose to undistracted attentiveness to this aspect of our environment. Still, the very fact of possessing the desire for true knowledge would seem to guarantee ultimate success.

In the end we shall find it unnecessary to rehearse each item of the exercises having to do with the sun. Sometimes a brief mental reference to the moods of wonder and grateful appreciation that the various times of day evoke will be all we shall need. As a result of the practice, wherever and however pursued, we may reap unexpected benefits. Even before going on to any of the exercises related to the self, we may begin to open ourself to the presence of spirit simply in intensifying our contact with the sun and its world. Our attentiveness to the reports of the senses, normally and allowably sensuous or at best aesthetic at first, should gradually begin to hint of the near presence of that third component which weaves the worlds of both sun and self into this forever new, moment-to-moment experience of the moment that is now.

* * *

Before taking up any exercises connected with the self, we may remind ourselves briefly of what the self means for us individually. Several facts about it are deeply impressive.

It was the sun that made possible the solar system in which we live and the life upon earth that has continued unbroken through vast stretches of evolutionary development. Ultimately it made possible the consciousness and self-awareness that evolved out of primitive biological existence. Nevertheless, in another sense it is the self (and the world it stands for) that has revealed the fact of the universe itself, and even the very fact of the self's own presence and functioning. If the sun is responsible for the evolving on earth of self-awareness and other-awareness, it is our own self that has revealed that fact to us. It is our self that reveals that the sun has enabled the cosmos to "know itself." It is our self, besides, that creates and reveals all the infinitely varied human relationships we enjoy, all our aesthetic, moral, and intellectual reactions to our world of experience. In this sense the self, too, is a teacher and deserves grateful recognition.

Had there been no self-awareness, even the mystical experience that first took the early Hindu sages beyond the self to the Oversoul, and the scriptural revelation and faith that turned the attention of men and women, East and West, toward the personal God, could not have manifested themselves. All would have been a mere blank. The self is in no way the *source* of the Oversoul or of God, of the divine spark in the soul or the divine power behind the physical creation. But only through the grace of the self, as it were, do we know not only of them but of our physical and psychic presence here and of the whole evolutionary process of life and consciousness.

One other fact about the self should be enough to produce a deep respect in us for what we seem to carry around with us inside our minds. Besides piercing beyond our own galaxy of perceivable names and forms on the gross material level to another such galaxy of atoms and subatomic particles within the physical universe we know, the self has helped the human mind pierce beyond the galaxy of thoughts and feelings and reactions to another such galaxy of unconscious drives and archetypal images within the mental universe we know. We cannot hope, most of us, to have a clear understanding of the fine structure of the mind, any more than of the fine structure of matter. But we *can* understand and appreciate this much: besides teaching us about the development of the solar system and of life and self-awareness, the self helps us, like the sun, to go beyond itself. This symbol of the second aspect of our environment leads directly to experience of spirit. Before our intuitive thinking about the self becomes second nature, we may find it useful to remind ourselves of these ideas daily.

Here again, the central practice will be to accustom the mind to experiencing the self, and later each mental object we encounter, as a *present fact*. To train the mind to know the self in this way, we may make it a habit to greet the self at several crucial points during the course of the day—first when we awake in the morning, then at midday, then at sundown, and finally when we go to bed. Obviously this kind of greeting is not quite the same as our greeting of the sun, for it is the self, as it were, who greets the self. The process of greeting, which amounts to what I have referred to just now as experiencing the self as a present fact, is simply to withdraw the five senses from all sides and let it affirm itself directly. But the greeting is to be done in such a way as not to treat it as an object, that is to say, to see that the sense of the self's presence is unaccompanied by thought images.

When we (as ego-self) become aware of the self in the morning, we may wish to greet it, after first greeting the sun, with wonder and love. We should try to think not that we ourselves *are* this or that sensation or feeling or thought that the self happens to be entertaining, but that it is because of the self's presence that these subjective motions are alive in us. We may even imagine, if we take the fancy, that the sensations and feelings and thoughts are turning about the self, irradiated by the self, and that it is the motionless self (as mediator of spirit) rather than these motions that is "here." As psychic cause of everything nonmaterial (that is to say, everything mental) in us and our psychological world, and as energy-pulsing source of its activity, the self's presence may be accounted as true center of our inner environment.

We may try to feel a quiet gratitude for the self's presence and for what we owe it in our interpretation of the objective world around us as well as of the subjective world within us—simply everything we perceive—and for its wakening us to a new day. If at any time the mind is clouded by anger, lust, or any other strong emotion, our sense of the self's presence may be momentarily lost to intuitive thought and we may revert to the same sort of forgetfulness that makes so many of us habitually put it out of consciousness. But here it is not as difficult to retrieve awareness of it as it is of the sun when it is covered by clouds. The clouds in this case only apparently divert us from it, for they never really come between us and it. At such times we may repeat mentally or aloud some text having to do with the individual self as referred to in scripture (the Bhagavad Gita, for instance, or, though less clearly, the New Testament). Or we may simply think of the thoughts about the self we considered before taking up these exercises.

As a reminder, I myself sometimes read a poem I wrote after visiting the Castalian Spring at Delphi, in Greece, at the foot of Mount Parnassus:

AT THE SPRING

The watcher at the spring—
Need he become
Each moving thing he looks upon?
Need he forget, even momently,
The thing he is,
And be the dancing sands he sees
Filter and whirl
Through the rock's thin opening,
Or the turned currents of
Light-catching waters as they pour
Upward and outward, churning through
A gathered water's depth and weight,
Or the half-yielding
Heads of small red water plants
Which ring the pool above
Its bed of gravel-spread limestone?

Why should a watcher so become
Wedded in thought
To any or to all of these

When, if he lies
Still and looks straight down,
With eyes uncaught by any thing
They meet—by dance
Or whirl or leafage or light-play—
Down through to the last sight,
Whichever of them he may see
Will point him always to the source
From which the waters and
The moving sand
Pour, churn, expand with undeterred
Sheer force, where no man need become
Anything other than he is.

As the sun in its nowness, irradiated by the primal energy, is not an abstraction, so the self in its nowness, irradiated by spirit, is not. Both of these are difficult to look at in themselves—and the self even more so than the sun, for the self is always visibly at "noon" for us (even in dreams). Thus the self, no matter how closely we observe it, will not regularly take on for us the widely different aspects that the sun appears to take on during the course of the day because of the earth's rotation. It will only be momentarily (and unpredictably) obscured by identification with egoistic thoughts, which vanish as soon as they are understood for what they are. We should therefore not try to form any picture of it, as I have already suggested. Still we may greet it variously, if we like, at several other points in the day.

At midday (after first greeting the sun) we may wish to think briefly of the self's awesomeness and the implications of our relationship to it. Whether we are to think of it thus, as we do of the sun, is for each of us individually to judge. We may allow ourselves to feel awe before it (in ourselves or in others) only so long as we are not tricked into seeing the self as an object. Even as a mere object, the sun is almost unthinkable simply because of its magnitude: how can anyone imagine a ball of fusing hydrogen-atom nuclei that is 864,000 miles in diameter and 2,700,000 miles in circumference, and 2.16×10^{27} tons in mass? If this is so, the self as experience—not conceived as subject as opposed to object, but immediately present—is totally unthinkable. Realizing that the very fact of our being able to experience it is part of the meaning of self-awareness, we should try at this moment of midday to grasp the self for the mystery it is.

As I have already pointed out, it is harmful to let thought about the self usurp a great portion of our time. Our daily life has to be pursued with diligence and alertness. Yet is is not unhealthy to steep the mind for a few moments at midday in the intuition of the self as vivified by the all-revealing spirit. Perhaps midday is as good a time as any to contemplate the fact of the presence of a self in all living beings, and preeminently (as we think) in human beings because of our self-awarensss.

Because it is intrinsic to our nature, we too often take the self, like the sun, completely for granted and overlook the miracle it represents: opportunity for participating in the physical world and the psychological world by an identity that at one and the same time is self-aware and plays host to an awareness (spirit) that *knows* it exists, that it is aware, that it loves. This identity is that through whose presence the thought "I perceive" is associated with the perception "sun," "star," "flower," "food," or anything else. As conduit or mediator for spirit, it is that which allows not only the sense of object and knowing subject to arise, but the "aftersense" of their union during fully realized normal experience. (To accept these intellectual fictions as real is the only way we can carry on our everyday thought and communication. In the end, we may come to see them as more than mere fictions.)

Again, at sundown we may greet the self and feel grateful for its presence—without, however, feeling gratitude *to it* as something outside ourselves, or even to what makes its presence as subject an intuitive experience, that is to say, spirit. What we should feel grateful for is the awareness of the miracles of perception and mental reaction that the working of spirit makes possible through it. If some such exercise is performed before going to sleep, we may bid farewell to the self as associated with waking consciousness, and all that it implies, in confident expectation that it will attend our waking in the morning.

We may also recall the various moods, good and bad, that the self has made possible during the day just past and check up on those occasions when they influenced our behavior adversely toward others. To feel personal animosities or other divisive emotions against those who have injured us or sought to injure us, or who do not appeal to us, or even who merely seem to dislike us, is to disregard the working of spirit in their selves. On the other hand, we may recall with love and thankfulness those friends or other persons (and all varieties of living creatures) with whom we come in contact daily, or have come in contact in the past, and especially those from whose contact we have derived unusual consolation or other benefit. Such thinking may be extended to the great creative spirits in history who have contributed to our aesthetic, intellectual, moral, or spiritual well-being.

If we are awake at midnight or near midnight, we may recall the presence of a self in all beings and picture these selves as innumerable outlets for the irradiating spirit, like a vast galaxy of interrelated lights. For it is spirit that in its creative functioning weaves them and their material worlds into one whole—both the nondual cosmic (including microcosmic) whole that all of us assume is there for us to experience and the whole that each of us realizes in our best moments.

These exercises, too, are all to be practiced with a view to seeing things as precisely as we can. In the world of sensation and feeling and thought, no point of view can hope to present things precisely as they are. Yet to carry on a mental life at all, we have to accept things as they present themselves to us for observation (at least those of us who observe the environment with normally healthy senses and mind). And we can learn to recognize where our estimates of the self are based on mental delusion and where they are not. Where, for instance, we see it as a separate something identified with anger, lust, and so on, or again with the idea of being the doer of deeds, and where we recognize its presence intuitively as the experience "I am," "I am aware," "I love."

If some of the exercises concerned with the self prove congenial and take hold of us, we may make contact with the self whenever we like during the course of the day. Such contacts may be made at almost any time, since they do not require our moving from wherever we are. And if the self becomes as real for us, in its own way, as the sun is, these contacts, too, will serve as a powerful source of inspiration. Meanwhile, at appropriate times we may also turn our attentiveness to the infinitely various workings of the mind—whether taken in relation to the rest of the mind or observed for themselves. This is a slightly more difficult discipline. But in time we can invent ways for ourselves, all the way from being alert to the reluctance with which we leave bed on a cold morning, to the anticipation with which we look forward to having something other than a sandwich at lunch with a prospective customer, to the sense of discouragement we may feel on confronting a philosophical concept too subtle for us.

As with the exercises having to do with the sun (and the senses), none of these should be allowed to interfere with our legitimate duties. If any of them seems too introverted for our own particular temperament, it may be discarded once we have become aware of it as a possible and legitimate concern for some other person.

At last, by gradual stages, we may become more or less continuously (though again not prepossessingly) aware of the self in the stillness of its Now. The result, as in the case of the sun, should be a far richer identification than we had known before with all the sensate and feeling and thinking beings about us. To know the self as person, far from shutting us off from others and making us introverts, should produce an identification with the concerns of other selves. The working of spirit through the self is responsible for whatever can speak to us—self to self—in plants, insects, fishes, reptiles, birds, animals, humans. The more naturally these relations develop, the more rewarding they will prove. It is for the individual man or woman to discover those aspects of the world that he or she can have meaningful relationships with—and those with which relationships have already been established unawares.

All these exercises can be practiced at any time and place, and as easily in the city as in the country. What we aim at, here too, is not simply to be aware of the self more or less continuously, but through it to be potentially aware of all that depends on it—in ourselves and others. The goal is to be intuitively in touch with whatever presents itself each moment in our immediate world of the self. What follows from the exercises may surprise us even more than what follows from practicing the exercises associated with the sun. For through them we become open in a far deeper sense to the working of spirit.

It is the assumption behind this book that very many average men and women without a definite religious faith nevertheless feel the need of a surer grounding in actuality than they now enjoy. Not a few of them may find that a program of attentiveness to the sun and the self as already outlined will suffice for life. Most of us, indeed, may find that our requirements are satisfied by use of the exercises described in this and the preceding section, or ones similar to them devised by ourselves. Few men or women are in any sense mystics, and the rest of us have little desire to follow a course of mental training like that undertaken by true mystics, a training involving long and deep concentration upon an objective or subjective ideal through exercise of will. We do not seek a breakthrough into the "x" behind the physical universe or the "y" behind the psychological universe. Our aim is simply to awaken a sense of full or nearly full participation in the now-and-here experience.

What impedes our full participation in day-to-day living is simply identification of the true *I* with the self-serving demands of the ego-self (to adopt for the moment the commonly held fiction that the ego is something autonomous and not merely a manifestation of thought). And the program we have reviewed so far, if adopted imaginatively and selectively by anyone with a lively desire to see things as they are, and practiced faithfully, can only attenuate the sense of a self-determined ego—though more gradually, of course, than would a program of yogic or other mystical disciplines.

* * *

We come next to exercises associated with spirit. As noted in the previous chapter, when we try to ascertain and feel appreciation for what spirit means to us, we are faced with a real difficulty. Even to remind ourselves of what the sun or the self means to us individually, we must withdraw the mind from whatever degree of awareness of our immediate environment we usually enjoy, for the process involves an intellectual abstraction. In view of this, how much more difficult it is when we presume to think about what spirit's immediate working means to us.

The sun and the self may be accepted as legitimate subjects for attention, each after its own fashion, in everyday thinking. We cannot conduct our life normally unless we treat them so. As we have already observed, we can also, in a manner of speaking, think *around* spirit. We spent some time in the previous chapter reminding ourselves of some of the workings of spirit that are especially significant for us; this we did so as to make ourselves feel more at home with it. We can extend the practice by forming the habit of observing each object or event that we encounter as being the result of spirit's working while it is being experienced. But how can we think directly *of* that which makes it possible to entertain, and bestows power on the self to experience, indeed to *be,* the intuition "I am," or "I am aware," or "I love"? I shall therefore not suggest here any thoughts about spirit. Rather, I shall assume that if we attend to the sun and the self, and their worlds, we shall by degrees acquire the needed openness to know spirit's presence and respond to it in each object or event we may experience.

There is one practice, however, that most of us might profitably adopt in connection with spirit. Whenever we are being attentive to sun and self (whether at dawn, midday, dusk, bedtime, midnight, or any other time), we may pause a moment or longer to touch them at one and the same time and, as we do so, feel receptive to that which, as it were, weaves their worlds into one. We may tell ourselves we do this so that if spirit is ready to unveil its presence and working, we will be ready to embrace it in its Now. For the religiously minded such a mood would amount to a "waiting on God," an expectation of God's coming. We might call it a state of nonanalytical alertness, a state where intellect is held in abeyance and healthy intuition takes its place—not the prescientific mood of a child or a primitive but rather a postscientific though childlike mood. This mood may sometimes possess us at times when we are not consciously trying to open ourselves to it.

We may also, at times, seek the desired openness to spirit through attentiveness to the sun or the self separately. If we choose to do so, our meditative concentration may appear to be a going toward spirit *through* the sun or *through* the self. Such a practice cannot be effectively carried out where there are many distractions. There is no doubt that the best place is one where we can quietly sit and look at the sun or be present to the self. Those who live in a city may find, if they can, a secluded spot in a park or devise such other means as they can to assure that they will not be interrupted. I myself, since I am living in the country, often wait until evening for a more extended practice and choose a seat near my garden. At such times, if a passive mood holds sway, as one devotes the attention to the sinking sun it may appear as if the world of the sun, the objective physical world, is all that there is. One is, as it were, at the center of a watchful whole that engulfs one. At other periods of the day an active mood may hold sway. At such times one may find that the watchful self engulfs the whole. These passing experiences are intuitional echoes, perhaps, of the more intense though not yet definitive experiences of mystics.

What we are aiming to obtain, finally, is neither a passive nor an active state, but one that balances the two. A state where we are aware not only of the world of the sun or the world of the self as they immediately present themselves, but of spirit interfusing them equally and breathing life into their continuing process. It is a state that requires of us no retiring into solitude and meditation and that is therefore the result of grace, inflowing into our readiness when the time is ripe.

In such a state, whatever happens to us by way of sense experience and of reaction on the part of others, or whatever creative inspiration floods the mind, is realized to be spirit speaking to us through them. Moreover, with each action we perform, each thought we think, each pleasure we enjoy, each emotion we feel, we are led to pay closest attention to the act done, the idea thought of, the pleasure enjoyed, the emotion felt—with little or no sense of separateness and yet with no loss of their or our own identity. We become intensely aware of the street we are driving through, or of the wood we are chopping, or of the words we are writing down, or of the mathematical problem we are helping a child to solve, or of the scent of the flower we smell, or of the taste of the food we are eating, or of the warm fondness or deep respect that someone's physical presence arouses in us. At the same time, the self experiencing it remains equally open to intuitive scrutiny. And all this without subtracting from our participation in the total situation of which we are a part.

We noted earlier that even mature mystics can hardly describe the content of their mature experience. Perhaps the intuitive experience I have been speaking of gives a faint hint of their transforming vision. That we are even now occasionally capable of this degree of attentiveness persuades me that their egoless awareness is not, finally, beyond us.

TO SEE THEM

To see them as they are would be
Not to see them
But to be them:
How then break away
Out of the web that holds you fast
And bids attention only see them?
Break out of the words' net
That will not set you free
Into the living light
Of living sight?

How but forget
The very meshes of the net:
The words, the phrases, clauses,
Grammar, cadences, and pauses—
Borrowed, begged, or stolen,
Age on age,
Out of a dreaming mind
Too much enamored of its dream?

But how forget? How but distill
Mind and will
Into an emptiness that yet
Is more than all:
That watches and accepts
(But not defines, not glosses,
Not explains)
Each object, each event
In being's complement,
Losses no longer counting losses,
Gains no longer gains?

But to watch them still would be
Only to see them,
Not to be them,
Till the watcher came to see
With something more than a watcher's eye;
Till his seeing learned to pierce
Past his own identity
To creation's nameless core,
Where his seeing self has stood
From before the start of time,
Ageless, dateless,
And aware;
Know the breath that livens him
And the life that breathes in them
Wedded till the end of time
In perpetual interview:

Seeking nothing,
Nothing shunning,
Owning all yet nothing owning,
Taste the saps they're pulsing with;
Past all pretense of believing,
Taking freely,
Freely giving,
Find the substantive of faith
In coevalness with them.

Far is near
And near is far
When you see them as they are.

* * *

Practicing the various sorts of exercises suggested in this chapter, some readers may find—as I myself have found at certain times in my life—that a regular routine of meditation is advisable, morning and evening. Anyone with a little imagination may compose his or her own.* Once we are established in a simple program of meditation, the more elaborate details of attentiveness to sun and self throughout the day may seem less urgently necessary. In that case we may lightly refer to them to whatever extent seems appropriate, whether before meditation or at other times. We should be careful to make sure that giving up our willed attentiveness is not the result of egoistic sloth but springs from a clear sense that exercise of will is no longer needed to guarantee awareness of sun and self.

There is a certain risk in setting out on the Road to Now, the spiritual journey, without authoritative guidance. Hitherto we have been thinking for the most part in terms suited to readers who have not found their truth in any of the established religious or philosophical traditions. It is up to such persons to make sure that their independence is the fruit of more than mere stubborn self-will. What I have suggested by way of discipline so far does not contravene anything that I myself have learned from those spiritual teachers I have studied with and heeded. If any readers feel inclined to heed them, they can probably assume that their spiritual approach does not spring from egoistic concerns. Even among such seekers, however, there may be some who will eventually feel a need for more precise and expert advice. In choosing a guide to whom they will give unquestioning obedience, they should first decide just what is their own temperamental need, and then, after familiarizing themselves with the sorts of teachers

---

*A tentative outline for such an exercise, based partly on the material already covered and flexible enough to adapt itself to varied temperaments, is given in Appendix A.

available to them, determine the qualifications of any teachers who present themselves.*

As the learning process advances, the real guide or teacher, the real agent of revelation, is recognized as just our own accumulated experience—perhaps better, time itself. This is another way of saying that in the end the mind becomes the teacher. When that happens the periods of attentiveness to the working of creative spirit become more or less continuous—as they did, for instance, for Brother Lawrence, a Christian monk. As Vivekananda once said describing this advanced state: "Know: I depend on no one, I have all I need, I no more need a teacher. All a guru is for is to teach us that we do not need a teacher." Then all that is left for us is to be and be aware, to love, and to act.

It will be a long time, for most of us, before we achieve anything like a continuous experience of this state of mind. And yet each time we obtain even a short taste of it, if our desire is sufficient and we are faithful to our purpose, the wait until its next rediscovery will almost surely be shortened.

Here are several practical hints about how to ease or enrich the period of relaxed striving: We may find that sometimes during the course of the day we cannot concentrate on what we are doing. We may feel dazed or even confused. Sometimes at night we may wake up and find that we cannot go back to sleep. There is no need to feel disturbed by such happenings. They may well be signs—at least, so I have often found—that just then the mind is ripe for a brief meditation on the sun and the self, and the interpenetration of their worlds as made one in spirit. After briefly meditating we should find that the mind is strengthened or relaxed, as the case may be, and we can then go about our work more efficiently or fall asleep readily.

We can encourage the mood of openness to spirit, as well, by regular reading of evocative literature in some quiet and secluded place—whether a city library or our own study or a sheltered garden. There are many helpful writings of mystics of East and West that should not be unpalatable to those to whom the recognized religious traditions do not speak. Best of all for those of a

*In Appendix B is a short discussion of various sorts of teachers.

more religious bent are perhaps the Epistles in the New Testament, read with intuitive understanding "from within" the Now experience (to the extent we are capable of doing so), or passages from the Gospel of John. If one's interests extend beyond the Christian sphere, the Bhagavad Gita or the classics of Taoism or even carefully selected passages from works on Zen are quite useful. And one can find many other meditative and evocative writings suited to one's own particular temperament. In such reading we should guard against imagining that *through* the reading we are grasping the presence of spirit. All we can do, if we read properly from within the Now experience, is make the mind receptive to whatever movings of spirit are presently available to us. Following such reading we may, if we like, practice a modest amount of attentive meditation. After such meditation, if we read. once again, we shall find that our intuition of the sense of the passages already read is clarified.

Through the methods we have been considering in this chapter we are aiming to elicit an unforced attentiveness to the living actuality of each successive moment—both outwardly in the world of physical objects and happenings and willed acts, and inwardly in the world of perceptions and feelings and plannings. In this practice of ours we are in a sense making the end the means and the means the end. By reproducing the conditions experienced by the mature mystic *after* his or her return from the heights—alertness to the immediate environment as one in spirit, without an illusory awareness of an independently separate ego-self or of outer and inner environment as absolutely separate entities—we remove the obstacles we have unknowingly erected to realization of what is already available to us each moment. Such obstacles include misguided expectations of some revealing insight in the future or false assumptions about our own inability, as a separate ego-self, to realize actuality now. At the same time, by focusing our whole attention on the practice, we find increasingly clearly in that very practice the end we are seeking. And as it thus becomes more and more spontaneous, we approach nearer and nearer to mature insight into Now.*

*A few further remarks about the experience of the mature mystic and its implications for average humans are given in Appendix C.

If ever we are tempted to think that both method and goal are wildly impractical—a temptation most of us will often be faced with—we need only remember the inescapable fact of death. What our everyday life entails, the seeing of constantly changing objects and happenings as somehow self-sufficient, would without that remembering seem the only true vision of what is real. But what death entails, a sudden end to our personally interpreted world of the senses and our inner world of imaginings, should forcibly remind us that to try to know actuality *now* is the height of practicality. To know actuality now means to know it not as something absolutely separate, not as something to be thought about or even to be "attained," but as something part and parcel of oneself and of the world, something that is not going to come to an end or escape us ever again. Knowledge of it is what human life is all about and should be our central concern as humans. Recognition of death's inevitability should help us keep all the "realistic" values of everyday life in perspective, without at all lessening their importance for us as present realities. Besides, we need only look receptively at the unclouded sun or at the self mysteriously housed here in our body to recall that, whether we will or not, we are even now face to face with actualities more instant than the most "real" and pressing of life's ego-serving concerns.

It should be clear by now that with the attenuation of ego-centeredness that inevitably comes with progress toward such a goal, goodness and moral behavior are also inevitable. Their place in the scheme of things becomes evident. Perhaps many of us assume that the reason we instinctively feel goodness and morality to be admirable and right is that they are indispensable for preserving a healthy human society—not to mention their being indispensable for communing with ultimate reality or God. Undoubtedly goodness and moral behavior are bound up with both. But our instinctive sense of their rightness actually springs from another source. It springs from the fact that when we live up to our best intuitions, when we are fully open to the Now of spirit, we cannot do evil, we have no reason to do evil. Even in our normal everyday life we instinctively feel that what is called good or moral is right because it is—whether in the form of good deeds or generous speech or moral thinking—an affirmation of the indivisible wholeness of existence. And this fact accounts for our sense of the rightness of trying to be ecologically responsible and to feel concern for racial justice and women's rights and the needs of the helpless poor. But as the sense of ego becomes increasingly attenuated, goodness and moral behavior become more and more spontaneous.

True, good qualities and good behavior may be used artificially, just as we use a willed attentiveness to sun and self, to reproduce the conditions for openness to spirit and so predispose us to receiving the gifts of spirit consciously when they offer themselves to us. To faithfully simulate the physical and mental attitudes that accompany a certain state of awareness is to invite the presence of that state of awareness. But as long as our goodness and our moral behavior—private as well as public—spring merely from imitation or fear, they do not yet indicate mature virtue unhampered by concerns of the ego-self.

Our path, then, is one that anyone with a little generosity of spirit and a little imagination can follow. It is a path far more gradual than the mystic's and therefore not nearly so perilous. But to follow it asks no less dedication than to follow the mystic's more austere and forbidding one. It is easier, though, in that with a reasonable amount of practice during a sufficiently long period of time the mind itself—with the help of spirit—begins to encourage the seeker. From time to time it unveils fresh intuitions that reveal new and undreamed-of vistas. Besides, a seeker on our path is not faced with the bleak desolations of ego and dark nights of the soul that the mystic faces in raising his or her will to the pitch needed for a heroic breakthrough into the "x" or the "y" behind the world of the sun or world of the self. It is a far gentler path and so it is less likely to tempt the ego-self to exploit it for its own devious purposes. Even highly advanced souls face temptations. As the observant Ramakrishna once said, "The pride of a saint in his saintliness is hard indeed to wear away."

✲ EPILOGUE

In this changing world of ours that we see and hear and touch and taste and smell, that we think about and enjoy and otherwise react to, is a revelation of spirit and its creative working. Each object we perceive, each happening we become involved in, each person we encounter in our immediate physical world, each thought we conceive, each sensation or feeling or reaction we savor in our immediate mental world, brings us a direct message from spirit itself. And these messages speak more persuasively, for us, than any other of the "goings-on of the universe" in the infinitely vast or the infinitely small or the deeply subliminal, because their message is spoken to us *directly*.

Almost everyone instinctively assumes that we know, or can know, the physical world around us—that part of our environment which makes up our Now of the sun—as it really is. I myself take this for granted most of the time. The assumption may not often reach the conscious level, but if I look carefully I find it always lying hidden there. And I am convinced that most others take the same thing for granted. The thought seems to be built into our very nature. Without it we should not be the persons we are.

When I look directly at the world within—that part of our environment which makes up our Now of the self—I take it equally for granted that we know, or can know, it, too, as it really is. This assumption probably reaches the conscious level less often than our assumption about the physical world, but it too seems to be built into our nature and helps make us what we are. Every moment of our waking life, instinct tells us that we are more or less fully in communion with the world of discursive thoughts, of reactions to sensations in the form of likes and dislikes, of emotions, memories, hopes, plans, beliefs, logical inquiry, as it really is.

The physical world, of course, includes more than the world available to our senses. Who of us nowadays does not speak with some assurance of atoms and molecules, of finer particles, even of galaxies, light years, an expanding universe? Or about the twentieth-century revelations of chemistry and physics, and the mysteries of biological evolution—indeed, of the substance of all the wide-ranging hypotheses of physical scientists? Though almost none of these things can be grasped by the unaided senses, we are convinced they are there. We feel we are somehow in touch, actually or potentially, with all that lies beyond immediate perceptions as well. Somehow we feel they, too, are real and that we know them, or can know them, as they really are.

Nor is the mental world simply what we encounter in our everyday experience. Psychology and psychoanalysis, as we have reminded ourselves in these pages, reveal that the surface consciousness is by far the smaller part of our mental processes. We do not experience those areas of the mind hidden beneath the surface—much as the fine particles of matter are hidden within perceivable matter—as we do our conscious thoughts and feelings. Yet when I think of it at all, I instinctively take for granted, as I believe others do, that I am in intimate touch with the whole flow and churning of a real subsurface activity. Even that part that I am not consciously aware of is, I assume, really there and somehow helps determine the more conscious activity of which I am or can be aware. It is not mere imagination.

Compelling as the totality of the world hidden from us can appear, it cannot compare in significance with the world that is ours, now and here. It is now and here that for each of us spirit is fully and perpetually at work; now and here that the three-dimensional designs of thought and feeling and emotion emerge into the four-dimensional world of space-time; now and here that the miracle takes place of the marriage of the world of the sun and the world of the self in the real and indivisible Now of spirit. It is the surface world, after all, that we deal with in everyday experience as our real world, and in which, when all is said and done, we find whatever salvation we may.

Because this is so, because the act of creation goes on observably now and here, it is *here* that each human being must return—whether from scientific inquiry or philosophic speculation or mystical ecstasy or flights of aesthetic rapture, or from memory or fancy—to live out and fulfill his or her creative human destiny. From any world beyond, or other than, the world of the senses and the conscious mind reacting to it, there is always a return to actuality so long as life lasts. That world, to be sure, may be irradiated, for the fortunate, by those other areas of experience. But to assert that ultimate reality is to be encountered somewhere else than here is to cut at the root of all the normal assumptions that make us human—and to deny the credibility of the very one making that assertion.

It is this fact of the necessity of return that underscores the all-importance for salvation, for communion with Now, of the common-sense experience and the common-sense view of our twofold world. It argues that ultimate reality, *for us,* is not the hidden noumenal world, but is the One World that flowers from that conjectured world, and from which alone we infer it. It may be this noumenal world that each of us sees in his or her unique way and that perhaps spirit knows in a final way. But the immediate reality, for humans, of the changing world we live in and think in is what all our inborn faith points to. Our profound intuition to this effect—our perennial assumption that we know reality when we come in contact with the phenomenal worlds of the sun and the self—tells me that humanity, with all its failings, is on the right track.

This is by no means to suggest that the common-sense view of the world, as it first appears to us, is sufficient. Following our native instinct, it is true, we must take the world of the sun and the world of the self to be real *as we perceive them*—and so, too, the sun and the self. But only as they are known truly. To know the sun truly we need not try to *see* the sun as a mass of fusing hydrogen-atom nuclei: that is impossible, however fascinating it may seem to the scientifically minded. It is enough to see it as the dazzlingly brilliant ball of incandescence that we perceive with the naked eye. But this does not mean that we must also believe that it actually rises in the east or crosses the sky or sets in the west.

That would be to remain victims of an illusion: the first view may be incomplete, but the second is incorrect.

In much the same way, we need not try to *see* the self in its function as focus of thought-energy and feeling-energy, or as conduit of spirit. But this does not mean that we should believe it to be the whole of our inner environment, enclosed in the body, or even identify it with the ego-self, the flow of egoistic thoughts that we habitually take it to be. That would be to remain victims of as great an illusion. Still, we have to speak of the sun as rising, of the self as "hungry" or "busy" or the like, simply to communicate with others. We have to speak of the world of the sun and the world of the self as separate entities, and of spirit as working alongside of or even within these two. So long as we know what we are doing when we speak in this way, we are quite safe. The words are suspect only when given absolutely literal value.

Our aim throughout this book has been to learn to live attentive to the surface world of the senses as our real objective world, but also to see it correctly—with the sun standing still in relation to the earth. Our aim has been to learn to live attentive to the surface world of the mind as our real subjective world, but seeing it, too, correctly—with the self "standing still," that is to say, no longer identified with the movements of ego-thoughts. Only if this is understood can we claim to be seeing things as they really are. Once it is understood, we can then intelligently make use of the worlds of the sun and the self to prepare ourselves for taking part in the flow of things as they are. As the only areas where we can expect to achieve openness to spirit, they are the only proper field of action for us as normal, average human beings.

There are those who hold that to accept the surface world of the senses and of the mind as our real world is to remain victims of the final illusion. Ultimate reality, they insist, cannot be known here: like the Egyptian god Amon, it must be "hidden" to be real. This is a very attractive idea, for it offers the hope of a final escape from the unsatisfactory aspects of the world as naively experienced. The ecstatic experience of certain types of mystics may seem to corroborate this view. But as we have noted, these mystics do not include those whom we may call mature mystics, who return to ordinary conscious life, now beholding *in and through* the surface world of senses and mind the reality they have intuitively known. Only those who are not fully mature human beings are persuaded it is hidden—only those who mistake Moses' "devouring fire" on the mountain, veiled in a cloud, for the true and perfect light. It is a fallacy, to my way of thinking, to take the hidden light to be more real than the light poured forth for humankind in the valleys of everyday life. The light is being constantly offered: it is we who cannot or will not open our eyes to it.

Jesus of Nazareth once taught his disciples with a parable about setting a lamp on a lampstand rather than placing it under a bushel basket. Christians often interpret his words as referring only to letting our light "shine before men." But the Gospel of Mark includes a telling variation of the parable. There Jesus is reported as saying, "For there is nothing hid, except to be made manifest; nor is anything secret except to come to light." And he adds, "If any man has ears to hear, let him hear."

The world seen in the Now of spirit is that hidden light made manifest. It is the secret understood. Nothing will have been added, really, when full openness to spirit dawns in us. Only our angle of vision will have changed from the point of view of an ego-trapped, ego-centered consciousness to the expanded awareness of the "true light that enlightens every man"—the light whose center is everywhere and in that sense is "your light," which should indeed "shine before men" as Jesus asked men and women to let it shine.

Once we are fully open to the Now of spirit, our daily life becomes for each one of us, even without our leaving our own house and our own friends, a continuous adventure into the unknown and yet familiar realm of spirit. As our attentiveness increases, we discover how refreshing it is—unexpectedly so—to be living simply from hour to hour, from moment to moment. Though we may be enjoying a well-regulated and safe life, we do not really know at any one instant what will happen next. Habits of thinking and of behavior may provide us with a design by which we imagine we can foretell just what we are to do or what is to happen to us the next minute, the next hour, or the next day. But actually we do not know what will happen to us or what we shall be called upon to do, even in the next instant. We ourselves may not always think of our new life in terms of adventure, for most of the time we shall be wrapped up in doing the adventuring. Indeed, it is part of the adventure, once we become aware of it, to see even forgetfulness of our daily life's being an adventure as itself belonging to the adventure.

Lending strength to the sense of our life's being a constant adventure is the deeper penetration we now experience of a truth long taken for granted: that whatever happens to us is the outcome of an endless chain of happenings, and whatever we feel called upon to do, through duty or impulse, is the result of some past action or desire of ours, good or ill, or of a combination of these. Now we see that one of the central workings of spirit is the law of cause and effect. To willingly embrace this fact makes it possible, finally, to react in such a way to whatever happens to us or perform our actions in such a way as will bear no entangling fruit, good or ill.

A further working of spirit, and so a further part of the adventure, is the discovery that each temptation to yield to old habits of wanting or of imagining, each stirring of self-pity or other motion of the ego-self, each straying from attentiveness, can be a trigger to remembrance of our central purpose: devoted attention, in spirit, to whatever immediately presents itself, without or within, at any particular moment. When such an occurrence effortlessly associates itself, in the mind, with wholehearted gratitude for the remembrance, the force of old habits of wanting or of imagining is weakened. We are on our way to a moment-to-moment flowing with the work of spirit that can become self-perpetuating.

Not the least important part of the adventure—in fact, the most engrossing part of it—is the actual vivid realization that each sense object or happening we meet with is an encounter with spirit itself, each exchange with another person, a teaching by spirit. And seeing this clear truth, we understand that at last we are at home—where without knowing it we have always been. We walk then hand in hand with the sun and with the self, aware of our complete dependence on them as showings forth of creative power, aware of their dependence on us as channels of the awareness that is spirit.

Every moment all of us—all creatures that have life—are experiencing the presence of what is ultimately real to the utmost of our capacity. Each one of us, just as we now are. If we increase the capacity, become conscious participants in the flow of things, we shall experience more richly whatever is waiting to be recognized and known. The greater our felt need to increase that capacity, the greater will be the effort we expend to increase it. We might adapt the Marxist maxim to our own quest for Now, transposing it to say, "*To each* according to his capacity, *from each* according to his need."

But a poem says it all:

THE PEARL

Do you know the hour,
Do you know the place,
Where a man must reckon
Face to face
With his dream and his doom?
It is now, it is here:
Why are you always
Waiting for
The day that hides
Beyond tomorrow?
Why are you waiting
Even for the moment
Beyond this, oh, most
Magical moment?

What was the use
Of all the yearning?
What did you think
To find when the desperate
Turmoil was over?
Rest, or acclaim,

Or the healing trust
Of a lover? Was any
Rest, ever,
But in this unquenchable
Clamor? Was ever
Reward for toil
But in toiling harder?
Was ever a haven
Of trust and acceptance
But in release into
Now, unveiling
Depth of tenderness
Given and received,
Unsmirched by claims
Of particular love?

Now is the end
Of timeward striving,
Now is the light
At which faith
Is always arriving,
Now is the pearl
Beyond price—
Each day, each hour,
Alike to be bought
Only by fresh and
Full surrender
Of all you momently
Made your own:
Sealed, by grace,
In the ripening sense
That a heaven is already
Here, perpetually
New and intense.

Here begins the final stage of the Road to Now, where it comes
full circle and leads us back to the start. Where we realize that the
road itself is the goal—that all that achieving the goal consists in

is direct knowledge that in actuality we never had to seek for it anywhere. The goal we were seeking for throughout a lifetime is not elsewhere, but just where we now are. In this liberating knowledge, intensely alert to and intimately in touch with our immediate surroundings, we have at last become fully human.

✷ APPENDIX A

Daily Meditative Exercise

The following suggestions are intended only for one who, after practicing the exercises suggested in the text, finds that a meditative program seems advisable to establish the mind in the proper mood for living a life of attentiveness throughout the day.

When you are ready for meditation you may first sit, either cross-legged on a rug or pillow or upright in a straight chair, breathing in and out evenly to calm the mind. In this routine it is not necessary to sit in the difficult lotus position. Merely sitting in an easy position so as to be able to forget the body is enough. At the start of any attempt at meditation or prayer the mind becomes automatically indrawn for a short time, without any special effort. Taking advantage of this phenomenon, you may briefly concentrate on your personal spiritual ideal. Or you may simply observe the breathing: while observing it, you may think, "I breathe in [adding "purity" or "understanding," if you like], I breathe out [adding "impurity" or "delusion," if you like]." You may continue to think of your ideal or to breathe awarely as long as you feel unconstrained. When mental activity reasserts itself you may spend some time watching the mind's restless activity until it tires of its movements.

Once the mind is relatively calm and recollected, you may take up the following routine for daily mental discipline:

You may begin with a prayer or intention offering up to creative spirit (or to God, if you prefer) the deeds you are about to do during the coming day, or the deeds you have performed during the day just past. The prayer is to be addressed to creative spirit through whatever conception represents your best *idea* of it, or through an external embodiment of deity (such as Jesus or Krishna or some other spiritual ideal), or even through a photograph of a holy person whom you consider to be an embodiment of deity. The words, either spoken aloud, repeated with the lips, or expressed mentally, may go somewhat as follows:

> I offer you, Creative Spirit [or God], the results of all the work I shall do in the course of the day. May the results, good or bad, go to you. I shall not work for praise or fame or merely for money's sake. Through my work I shall serve only you.

At the close of the day you should substitute the phrases "have done" and "have not worked" and "have served" for those in future tense. Though addressing creative spirit as "you," you may remind yourself that the "object" of your prayer is not essentially apart from your own true self.

You may then send thoughts of well-wishing to all living things on earth—people, animals, plants—saying in turn to the North, to the South, to the East, to the West, above, and below:

> May all beings become peaceful, joyful, and contented.

You may think of your thoughts of well-wishing as proceeding uninterrupted in all directions in infinite space, or as encircling the earth.

Continuing in the same manner, you may send thoughts of love, good will, and harmony—with earnest feeling—to all creatures. You may picture them as best you can as dwelling in all parts of the globe, repeating words to this effect:

> To all the elements and compounds—love, good will,
>   and harmony,
> To all microorganisms and plants—love, good will,
>   and harmony,
> To all fishes and other water creatures—love, good will,
>   and harmony,
> To all insects, spiders, worms, and other crawling things—
> love, good will, and harmony,

To all reptiles—love, good will, and harmony,
To all birds—love, good will, and harmony,
To all animals, great and small—love, good will,
   and harmony,
To all men and women: black, brown, red, yellow, white,
in every part of the earth—love, good will,
   and harmony.

While repeating these words, if it helps to visualize them you may think of the various creatures in some detail, as they inhabit the earth. Human beings you may think of as they are distributed on the various continents. In all this, however, there should be no sense of constraint. If there is, the suggestion should be ignored or the whole practice omitted.

In the same strain you may continue:

To all friends, relatives, and acquaintances—love,
   good will, and harmony.

At this point you may think of those individuals, living or dead, who mean much or have meant much to you. You may briefly and feelingly touch them in thought as you picture them and repeat their names. Then you may proceed:

To all who strive for openness to creative spirit
   [or to God]—love, good will, and harmony,
To all whom I may injure [have injured] during the course
   of the day—love, good will, and harmony,
To all who may seek [have sought] to injure me during the
   course of the day—love, good will, and harmony.

Here you may think of the disregarded minorities or the helpless poor, some of whom you may have directly or indirectly injured by your indifference, and some of whom might wish to repay your indifference by doing violence to you or your kind. Also you may think of political leaders or others against whom you may find you habitually have a specially strong resentment.

If you have a spiritual director or someone whom you look upon as your guru, you may say:

To my teacher—love, good will, and harmony, that our study may be fruitful and there may be no misunderstanding on either side.

Here you may repeat the name not only of your spiritual teacher (or teachers) but that of any of the great figures in human history to whom you are grateful for enriching your cultural life. You may then think of the greatest spiritual figures of the world (or in your particular spiritual tradition) and say:

To the great spiritual lights of the world—love, good will, and harmony, that they may lead me to communion with creative spirit [or with God].

And finally:

To anyone whom I may have forgotten—love, good will, and harmony.

Before proceeding to meditate on the Now of spirit in the form of your own spiritual ideal, you may add here:

This mind is pure and strong: it is free from anger, passion, jealousy, hatred [or whatever passions most impede you]; it is full of love; it is open to creative spirit [or God].

This body is pure and strong: it is strong in every cell, in every fiber, in every tissue; it is a temple of spirit; through its help and the grace of creative spirit [or God] I shall realize the Truth in this life.

At this point you may make a resolute effort to withdraw the mind from discursive thought and concentrate it for some time on your spiritual ideal. Before you begin the concentration, you may if you like repeat the following adaptation of the Gayatri Mantra (originally used as a means of meditating on the sun as symbol of deity):

* * *

> I meditate on the glory of that Being who has produced this universe; who pervades earth, the heavens, and the space between; who is the power of the angels [or higher beings]; who is my innermost self. May he enlighten my consciousness.

(Several other versions of the prayer are given in the reference notes, and if one of them appeals to you more it may be used.)

After repeating this mantra you may begin the meditation proper. Meditation on a personal form of God may be done by visualizing God's form in the heart and trying to realize its meaning for you. Meditation on the transpersonal reality, by opening yourself to the Now of spirit (in the heart or head) and trying to empty the mind of discursive thought. Such meditations, if they are to be attempted in depth, are best learned from a teacher in one of the devotional or nondevotional Hindu traditions (or from a monk in a contemplative Christian order). For ordinary purposes, any procedure you may devise is acceptable so long as it is simple and allows the mind to become concentrated on your ideal. The aim of the meditation is to encourage a gradual illumination through ever greater openness to creative spirit, rather than to achieve a sudden mystical breakthrough.

Whatever practice you may adopt, the length of time spent in the meditation should be adjusted to your strength and not to momentary enthusiasm. The whole process from the beginning of the routine to the end of the concentration should be kept at the start within a half-hour. If at any point the mind becomes deeply concentrated, you may let it rest there and make that your meditation. If at any time your meditation is interrupted by an external sound, instead of fighting it you may concentrate on the distracting sound itself. At the conclusion of the meditation you may offer up whatever merit you have derived from the meditation to your objective or subjective ideal.

Because your goal is to enter more and more fully into awareness of the Now of spirit in the living moment, you may find it helpful after concluding the practice to sit still for a minute or two. You may breathe in and out regularly and relaxedly and think (with eyes open) of the fact of the objective world outside you and the subjective world inside you, reminding yourself that there is really no way of telling where either of them ends and the other begins. This is another way of saying that in the Now of spirit they are one and nondual, and there is no place where spirit is not. After rising from meditation, as you take up your various duties during the day, you may try to keep your mind attuned to the working of spirit, seeking to realize as far as possible your intimate participation from moment to moment in the living organic whole.

Remember: You should take up this daily meditative routine not because it has been recommended to you but only if it appeals to you and seems called for in your case. It does not lead to any more esoteric discipline nor is it designed to help you to a mystical breakthrough of any kind. It is not an end in itself, nor is it even necessary. Its sole purpose is to help those who wish to enrich their experience of the working of spirit by increasing their openness to it during each day. If it produces no such quickening, it should be dropped. I have no further suggestions to offer about meditation, nor do I advocate any one mantra (sacred formula for repetition) or any one ideal upon which to meditate. The central practice remains, now and always, your moment-to-moment facing each day, and all day, of the fact of the Now of the sun and the Now of the self and their union in the Now of spirit.

For readers who feel that they have become lukewarm in practicing their inherited religion, it may be helpful, before adopting any program of exercises, to abandon for a time *all* forms of spiritual practice and even of prescribed belief. One will then be living the relaxed life of a person who, though not an atheist (there are fewer of these than is generally realized), is yet without a specific religious faith. In this way the brain may be washed of a quantity of previous coloring: images and concepts that had perhaps led it to ignore the offerings of spirit in its direct experience through the senses and thought and feeling.

If the reader happens to be such a one, he or she may take comfort. All that is required is a sincere desire to know the presence of spirit as it reveals itself in the world of the sun and the world of the self, and so to realize more and more fully one's full human potentiality. In the end, the fitting discipline (either as suggested here or as found elsewhere) will make itself available— not just a discipline that one feels one *ought* to practice, but one that can be practiced enthusiastically because one *wants* to practice it.

✲ APPENDIX B

Types of Gurus

For learning an art or a craft or a profession—indeed, in preparing for any vocation—what we need is someone who can guide us toward proficiency. And it is quite the same for preparing to lead a spiritual life. The need for spiritual advisers has always been recognized by those seeking to lead a life of contemplation in a monastic order. Nowadays there is a demand among many leading a life in the everyday world—and especially among young people—for persons capable of guiding them. But there are different sorts of teachers, and it is necessary to know something about them if one is not to be disappointed and end up by feeling doubtful about the spiritual life itself.

There are various kinds of legitimate spiritual teachers or, as they are called in India, gurus. The superior type is said to be able to *transmit* spiritual insight with a look or a touch; another type *shares (with varying degress of success)* what knowledge he or she has gained through personal practice or learned from a superior teacher; and still another type simply *talks or writes* about what others have said and experienced. Each type is needed, for not all men and women are ready for a teacher of the first or even of the second type. Most people cannot expect to find a guru who can confer spiritual illumination directly, but they may hope to find one who has had some amount of practical experience. If one uses whatever discrimination one has been gifted with, one can usually avoid disappointment. A legitimate teacher is wholly or largely free from identification with the ego-self and always has the student's welfare at heart.

The fact that a person has accepted a spiritual teacher need not hold him or her bound for life. There may come a time when an earnest student finds that the teacher can be of no further help. The situation is not unlike that of a student seeking musical or other artistic instruction: sometimes, indeed, such a student proceeds from teacher to teacher. That is not necessarily a sign of instability. In this case the student merely outgrows the previous teacher—as, to take an example in music, Ludwig van Beethoven did—and seeks out another. The very same thing can happen with those who seek spiritual instruction. The saint Ramakrishna benefited from a series of gurus, and in turn became the teacher of several of his own teachers. Again, there are men and women who cannot accept any single religious authority or discipline as final. For them a time comes when circumstances prompt either a change of faith or a giving up of allegiance to any one specific faith. There are also those who have no faith. As I have pointed out, my writing of this book has been partly inspired by the need of such persons for some sort of spiritual discipline.

There is no fixed time when we can expect to dispense with a spiritual teacher. In a trade like welding or bricklaying or carpentry one can look forward to an end of one's apprenticeship, when one will have mastered all the essential details of the trade and may set to work independently. But spiritual instruction is instruction in building a complete person. For many, a spiritual teacher may prove indispensable for the greater part of their lives—much as a professional singer may continue to use the services of a singing coach—and if they are lucky they will not have to change teachers. A guru is indispensable, though, only so long as we have yet to become somebody in our own right. We can always look forward to a time when, as Hindus say, the mind shall become the guru.

I mention all these matters to keep the record straight. Readers should not imagine that these suggestions, given by way of instruction, are to be taken as the infallible pronouncements of a superior teacher. I am certainly not a guru in the sense that I can confer spiritual insight or have realized everything I write about. But I have at least experimented with disciplines prompted by the intuitions that have been given me, and I have had the good fortune to have known gurus of no mean spiritual attainments and to have become the disciple of one of them.

The suggestions for discipline in the fourth chapter of this book and in Appendix A reflect only what I have found to be useful for myself after taking up my guru's suggestions or following my own intuitions. But they are presented in terms of personal experience that is available to any man or woman, whether believer or agnostic. They are intended to help readers fix their attention more steadily on the matters we have considered, matters already within their own immediate range of experience, and presumably, if they have read as far as this page, somewhat congenial to their own thinking. Wherever any of the practices conflict with a reader's accepted beliefs, they may be adjusted as seems advisable. If any reader makes them a substitute for original and increasingly adventuresome effort on his or her own part, my purpose will have been frustrated.

✳ APPENDIX C

Mature Mystical Experience

We have touched on the mystical witness of ancient Hindu sages in relation to the Oversoul (Atman) and to the Godhead (Brahman), and on the revelation of Krishna in the Bhagavad Gita. I have also mentioned the witness of the Old and the New Testament in relation to the "timeless Christ" and the Spirit of God, or Holy Spirit. Both witnesses seem to me to be bound up not only with genuine mystical experience but with the experience of the mature mystic *after he returns* to everyday consciousness. We should take time to reflect on the stage of consciousness that mature mystical awareness involves, for it has something to do with ourselves.

There are two sorts of genuine mystical experiences: "profound" mystical experience and "mature," or ultimate, mystical experience. They have not always been sufficiently distinguished by writers on religious mysticism. Profound mystical experience represents a realization of suprasensuous and supramental reality—what we have termed the "x" and the "y" behind the world of the sun and the world of the self. Bestowed on some few without previous preparation, it is usually achieved after a period of strenuous effort. But it is always bestowed through what devotional religions know as grace—the grace of a power beyond the individual. It occurs not *because of* the effort, in the sense that the effort creates it, but rather because the effort has removed obstacles to the awareness of what in actuality was already present though unrecognized. Writers on mysticism, Eastern or Western, sometimes suggest that this is the ultimate in spiritual experience. But it is not, I submit, always as final as it is claimed to be.

Even the undoubtedly intense experience of one who has been

granted a vision of the "x" or "y" behind appearances can remain a limited one. Far more persuasive than one's everyday sensing and conceiving of the objective and subjective worlds, it still remains an experience of the undifferentiated Oversoul or of the undifferentiated One, the "God beyond God." If the mystic stops there, his experience is hardly less abstract (that is to say, three-dimensional) than the experience of a fusing of the two worlds in our everyday life. Like it, the experience is seen (in retrospect) as something apart, something sacred. Like it, it comes to an end and becomes a memory—haunting, no doubt, and something to be yearned for, but no longer immediately present as actuality. This type of mystical experience, intense though it is, is by no means to be looked upon as a preview of what we shall enjoy in an afterlife. Coming to an end, as it does, it is not the true goal of the spiritual life. As the saint Ramakrishna once said: "Samadhi (profound mystical ecstasy) is only the beginning of the spiritual life."

Fully mature mystical experience, on the other hand, is a totally transforming experience. Like profound mystical experience, it may be received unexpectedly, without previous preparation. But it, too, is usually received after strenuous effort. Its difference lies in the fact that the experience is totally transforming. Like fully realized sense experience, though far more intensely, it is a four-dimensional experience. Mature mystics are those who, on their return to the everyday world, find there a more or less uninterrupted *continuation* of the experience of release from identification with the ego-self that they enjoyed in profound mystical ecstasy. Along with the greater balance that comes of any profound mystical experience, they exhibit utter but unobtrusive selflessness. Only such persons may be considered complete human beings.

It seems clear from some of the statements of certain of the early Hindu sages that they had achieved this mature mystical experience, as did, no doubt, modern Hindu saints like Ramakrishna and Ramana Maharshi. Christian mystics like the Apostle John and (by his own witness) Saint Paul certainly achieved it, as have many ancient and modern mystics in various other religious traditions.

It may also be observed that many seemingly nonmystical persons exhibit balance and selflessness, and sometimes a capacity for attentiveness, to an unusual degree. Though not so evident to casual observation, these qualities are no less firmly grounded than those same qualities in the mature mystic. Yet such persons seem to have practiced no disciplines to achieve a mystical breakthrough. Can we draw any inferences from the similarity? On the basis of reason as well as intuition, I conclude that the presence of spirit communed with by the mature mystic in everyday life is no less available, now and here, to persons who are not mystically gifted in the commonly accepted sense. Provided, that is to say, they have spent the necessary time in the school of everyday experience as seriously inquiring though active human beings and provided they feel sufficient desire.

If we recall for a moment my own series of youthful aesthetic experiences of the twilight sky, culminating in a final loss of the sense of time and place, the argument may become clearer. What I learned then, unknowingly, was that there is indeed something deeper than external beauty to which one can penetrate through complete (even though not always consciously willed) attentiveness—something that is always here beneath the bright surface of everyday sense experience and thought, as the starry sky is always there beyond the veil of dazzling brightness spread by the sun. Anyone alert to the working of spirit is aware of this deeper something as living *in and through* the world of the senses and of the mind. And this intuition has been corroborated for me by my later experience of longer periods of awareness of spirit's creative working.

In seeking to achieve full attentiveness to the environment around us and within us, and so become open to the Now of spirit, we are seeking to realize our full potentiality as humans. Experiences like those I have mentioned, and the example of persons who exhibit an effortlessness and natural balance and selflessness, give promise that by following a *natural method* we can indeed at last achieve the balanced attentiveness to the total immediate environment that we seek, which is the mark of the mature mystic. And this without having to pass through extraordinary mystical states. We aim to bypass all the specialized effort of the yogi or Zen monk or other mystic and come to the world view the mature mystic achieves *after* his successful return to everyday consciousness. We want to head straight for what Buddhist and Christian and Hindu and Sufi mystical writers keep on insisting is available to one and all, if they would only see it. We are taking them at their word.

�֎ NOTES AND REFERENCES

The references are to direct quotations on the pages indicated or, when marked with a ¶ sign, to material within the paragraph beginning with the italicized words following it. Author's comments on passages in the text may be introduced by this sign followed by the opening words of the paragraph referred to, or may simply follow references to quoted material.

PROLOGUE

3 ¶*This couple had*   Members of the Ramakrishna Order, founded about 1900 by the Hindu patriot monk Vivekananda, profess two ideals: worship of God through service of the poor, the suffering, and the illiterate, and direct experience of God's presence through meditation and prayer. Monks serving outside India—in Europe, the United States, and elsewhere—preach the doctrines of modern Hinduism, stressing the soul's intimate relationship with an all-embracing godhead, the oneness of the universe, and respect for the great religions of the world as ways of achieving communion with God. For a more detailed description of the order, see John Moffitt (ed.), *A New Charter for Monasticism* (Notre Dame: University of Notre Dame Press, 1970), pp. 153ff.

5 ¶*It was to bolster*   The Buddha and the Zen masters of China and Japan insisted that such an insight comes only after long and arduous spiritual struggle, as did the mystics of Vedic times before them. The Desert Fathers of early Christianity and subsequent contemplatives, Christian and Islamic and Hindu, underwent mortifying disciplines to that end. Yet the young man's experience is not the only example of someone who, when he was ready and the time had come, obtained a revealing insight without undergoing heroic discipline. To find striking examples of other seemingly unprepared persons who achieved a decisively transforming experience, one need only recall Saul of Tarsus, or Catherine of Genoa, or, in twentieth-century India, Ramana Maharshi. Less gifted but equally unprepared persons in the past may well have achieved at least a high degree of such insight—though the experience itself may not have been as continuous as theirs. The young man's having obtained some such insight would seem to indicate that ordinary ungifted persons may still hope to do so.

THE NOW OF THE SUN

11 Do not look at the sun   From *This Narrow World* (New York: Dodd, Mead & Company, 1958), p. 18.

14 ¶Throughout Egypt's history   For a few details in this paragraph I am indebted to Christiane Desroches-Noblecourt, *Life and Death of a Pharaoh: Tutankhamen* (New York: New York Graphic Society, 1963). In a later work, Cyril Aldred, *Akhenaten: Pharaoh of Egypt* (New York: McGraw-Hill Book Company, 1968), p. 261, the dates of the three pharaohs' reigns are conjectured as follows: Akhnaton, 1378–1362 B.C.; Tutankhamon, 1362–1353 B.C.; Ay, 1353–1349 B.C. In the present volume the spellings Aton and Amon are used, alone and in the pharaohs' names, in place of Aten and Amen or Amun.

O living Aton   For a full prose translation of this hymn, see Cyril Aldred, p. 187.

16 ¶This late poetic   For a few details in this and the following paragraph I am indebted to the work by Cyril Aldred mentioned in the two preceding references.

17 We meditate on the unsurpassed   Rig-Veda 3.62.10. The Sanskrit is as follows: *"Tat Savitur varenyam / bhargo devasya dhimahi / dhiyo yo nah prachodayat."* The conjectured date is about 1500 B.C. For help in wording the translation of this three-line verse (with eight syllables in each line), I have consulted Swami Nikhilananda (trans.), *The Upanishads*, abridged edition (New York: Harper & Row Torchbooks, 1963), p. 242, n. 154; L. R. Pandey, *Sun-Worship in Ancient India* (Delhi: Motilal Banarsidass, 1971), pp. 14–15; Jan Gonda, *Vishnuism and Sivaism* (London: Athlone Press, 1970), p. 73. I have sought advice also from K. L. S. Rao of the University of Virginia.

¶Evidence of sun worship   For the details about worship of the sun in this and the following paragraph, I am indebted to the work of L. R. Pandey referred to in the preceding note, pp. 1–9, 10–15.

18 ¶There are innumerable   The reference to Satya, the True, is found in *Brihadaranyaka Upanishad* 5.5.2. The date of this Upanishad is thought to be about 600 B.C.

The door of the Truth   *Isha Upanishad* 15–16. Quotations from the Upanishads in this volume are taken from Swami Nikhilananda (trans.), *The Upanishads* (ref. note for p. 17 above), and occasionally adapted for poetical reasons or for the sake of clarity. In line 6 of this invocation, the words "Lord of Creation" have been added. The words "Supreme Person" in the last line have been substituted for "Purusha."

19 ¶Formal sun worship   Details in the third sentence of this paragraph are derived from L. R. Pandey, *Sun-Worship in Ancient India* (ref. note for p. 17 above), p. xxx; a few in the remainder of the paragraph are from Alan Anderson, "Astroarchaeology," *Time* (September 3, 1973), p. 73 (a review of Gerald Hawkins, *Beyond Stonehenge* [New York: Harper & Row, 1973]).

19 The eye of the great god   This hymn to the sun is quoted by permission of the author from Barry Fell, *America B.C.* (New York: Quadrangle/The New York Times Book Co., 1976), p. 294, as is the information about the Iberian Celts immediately preceding it. The hymn was first collected by Alexander Carmichael in the nineteenth century.

20 Lord of the Close Vicinity   Assembled from quotations from Frances Gillmor, *Flute of the Smoking Mirror* (Albuquerque: University of New Mexico Press, 1949), p. 95.

20 ¶Among the Hebrews   For a reference to the sun, see also Psalm 19:1, 5–6. Quite as impressive as the parallels in Psalm 104 to Akhnaton's hymn is the psalm's opening: "Bless the Lord, O my soul! / O Lord my God, thou art very great! / Thou art clothed with honor and majesty, / who coverest thyself with light as with a garment" (Psalm 104:1–2).

21 true light that enlightens   John 1:9

Praised be my Lord God   "Canticle of the Sun," verse 2. From *Challenge* (Chicago: Loyola University Press, 1958), used by permission (translator unknown).

Hail the heaven-born Prince of Peace!   "Hark, the Herald Angels Sing," verse 3; from *The Hymnbook* (New York: Presbyterian Church in the United States, The United Presbyterian Church in the United States of America, Reformed Church in America, 1955).

22 ¶According to the estimates   For many of the details in this section I am indebted to Heinz Haber, *Stars, Men, and Atoms* (New York: Washington Square Press, 1966), pp. 60–69, 129–130; for a few, to Kenneth Weaver, "The Incredible Universe," *National Geographic Magazine* (May 1974); E. N. Parker, "The Sun," *Scientific American* (September 1975); and Frederick Golden, *Quasars, Pulsars, and Black Holes* (New York: Charles Scribner's Sons, 1976). I have also been helped by constructive comments on this section by John A. Wheeler.

23 ¶At the sun's core   For the diameter of the hydrogen atom, mentioned in the final sentence of this paragraph, I am indebted to James H. Otto and Albery Towle, *Modern Biology* (New York: Holt, Rinehart and Winston, 1965), p. 34.

24 ¶How the sun became   A current theory holds that the heavier elements may have been supplied by the explosion of a giant dying star (supernova) in the relative vicinity of the incipient sun. For a reference to this theory see Isaac Asimov, "Asimov's Guide to the Universe," *Focus* (June/July 1980), p. 32.

30 ¶The molecular structures   For a detailed account of evolutionary progress, see Julian Huxley, *Evolution in Action* (New York: New American Library, 1957), especially chapter 5.

32 convenient lies   See poem on p. 11.

33 golden disk   See quotation from *Isha Upanishad* 15–16 on p. 18.

Tireless you wait   This poem is first published here.

37 I love you—so fresh and still   First published here.

39 In blinding heat one summer day   From *Signal Message* (Francestown, N.H.: The Golden Quill Press, 1982), p. 29.
41 Quick, clear-eye, curve-bill   Ibid., p. 76.

THE NOW OF THE SELF

44 Looking in each face   Reprinted from *The Living Seed*, p. 29, by permission of Harcourt Brace Jovanovich, © 1962 by John Moffitt.

44 ¶The first works   The volumes containing these lectures by Vivekananda are titled *Jnana-Yoga*, *Bhakti-Yoga*, *Raja-Yoga*, and *Karma-Yoga*. They are included in *Vivekananda: The Yogas and Other Works* (New York: Ramakrishna-Vivekananda Center, 1953).

47 ¶An even more arresting   Besides the books on the yogas, I read at this time Vivekananda's *Inspired Talks* (also included in *Vivekananda: The Yogas and Other Works*, referred to in the preceding note), the fragmentary but fascinating record of talks with a few American disciples in 1895. Romain Rolland's *Life of Ramakrishna* (Calcutta: Advaita Ashrama, 1928), included also in his *Prophets of the New India* (New York: Albert & Charles Boni, 1930), is valuable as the response of a celebrated Westerner to this great modern Indian saint.

48 ¶I must add here   At this first meeting, the swami showed special concern about the extremes I had gone to in the breathing exercises. In his opinion the only reason I had not done myself great mental harm was that I had been practicing sexual continence. The remark related to a traditional Hindu monastic belief that chastity in thought, word, and deed is a prerequisite for mystical experience. It strengthens, Hindu monks say, the whole mental fiber and especially the memory, which is indispensable for faithful adherence to spiritual practice. Whether this notion is universally applicable may be questioned. I was once told by a deeply serious Japanese follower of Zen that sexual experience is allowable so long as it does not divert the mind from its goal. This does not entirely contradict the Hindu monastic teaching. For certain persons complete continence obviously frees the mind for deep plunges into mystical contemplation. Perhaps it is indispensable for the experience of oneness, what is known as "profound" mystical experience (see Appendix C). My own guess is that as a preparation for becoming open to mature mystical experience, where experience of oneness is accompanied by awareness of objects of perception and perceiving self, it is a matter of individual temperament.

49 ¶Acquaintance with the Hindu   For further details about the religious philosophy of Nondualism, see Swami Vivekananda's *Jnana-Yoga* (ref. note for p. 44 above); Swami Nikhilananda, *Hinduism: Its Meaning for the Liberation of the Human Spirit* (New York: Harper & Row, 1958); John Moffitt, *Journey to Gorakhpur* (New York: Holt, Rinehart and Winston, 1972), pp. 61–67.

50 ¶In one of the principal   Concerning the "sheaths" (*koshas*), see *Taittiriya Upanishad* 2.2.12ff.; see also Swami Madhavananda (trans.), Shankara, *Vivekachudamani* (Calcutta; Advaita Ashrama, 1966), pp. 47, 58. The ninth-century religious philosopher referred to in this paragraph is Shankara (A.D. 788–820). For a brief account of his life and thought, see *Journey to Gorakhpur* (ref. note for p. 49 above), p. 58ff.

51 ¶The separate individual soul   The two schools of thought referred to in the second sentence of this paragraph are represented by (among others) the Modal Nondualism of Ramanuja and the Dualism of Madhva. For details about Ramanuja (A.D. 1017–1137) and Madhva (A.D. 1199–1278), see *Journey to Gorakhpur* (ref. note for p. 49 above), pp. 101–105, 107.

51 law of karma   The law that prescribes, according to the Hindus, that each desire and each act associated with a selfish motive must bear fruit, good or ill. That fruit is reaped in either the present or a subsequent life by the individual who thus desires or acts. Through nonattachment to the results of previous desires or actions, the individual soul is freed from further results of his or her desires or actions.

    ¶To prepare ourselves   For many of the details of this and the three paragraphs following, I am indebted to J. D. Conway, *Facts of the Faith* (New York: All Saints Press, 1961, © 1959 by Doubleday & Company), pp. 26–29.

52 Let us make man   Genesis 1:26

53 ¶There is one notable   For information about the development of Christian ideas about the soul, see Elmar Klinger, "Soul," *Sacramentum Mundi* (New York: Herder and Herder, 1970), vol. 6, pp. 138–140; L. B. Puntel, "Spirit," ibid., pp. 142–145; M. Müller and A. Halder, "Person," ibid., vol. 4, pp. 404–409. Though a product of Roman Catholic scholarship, the international theological encyclopedia *Sacramentum Mundi* is marked by an openness toward the other Christian churches, the non-Christian religions, and the world in general. It is an attempt to formulate present-day developments of the understanding of the Christian faith, based on modern theological investigations. While it takes fully into account past and present growth in such understanding, it has also a marked orientation to the future.

54 ¶It was Sigmund Freud   For some of the details of this section, I am indebted to Benjamin B. Wolman, *The Unconscious Mind* (Englewood Cliffs: Prentice-Hall, 1968) and D. Wilfred Abse, *Hysteria and Related Mental Disorders* (Bristol, England: John Wright and Sons, 1966). I have also consulted Albert Gorres, "Psychoanalysis," *Sacramentum Mundi* (ref. note for p. 53 above), vol. 7, pp. 133–135; Erwin Ringel, "Individual Psychology," ibid., vol. 5, pp. 148–151; Raymond Hostie, "Depth Psychology," ibid., vol. 5, pp. 151–153. I have also been helped by constructive comments on this whole section of chapter 2 by D. Wilfred Abse.

54 ¶Carl Jung pushed   For the information in this and the next two

paragraphs, I am chiefly indebted to Joseph Campbell, "Editor's Introduction," *The Portable Jung* (Princeton: The Princeton University Press,
1971), pp. xxvi–xxviii.
55 ¶It was Jung who   For more on introversion and extraversion, see
V. E. Fisher, *An Introduction to Abnormal Psychology* (New York: The Macmillan Company, 1947), pp. 31–41.
56 ¶A few of Jung's remarks   The details of this paragraph are derived
from C. J. Jung, *Analytical Psychology* (Princeton: Pantheon Books, 1968),
p. 10.
56 ¶A statement of Freud's   The details in this paragraph are derived
from Sigmund Freud, *Traumdeutung* (trans. Brill, 5th ed., 1919), p. 486,
as quoted in William Brown, *Psychology and Psychotherapy* (New York:
Longmans and Company, 1921), p. 62.
63 The self-existent Supreme Lord   Katha Upanishad 2.1.1. From Swami
Nikhilananda (trans.), *The Upanishads*, (ref. note for p. 17 above). The
translation of the first sentence has been slightly adapted: the words
"when he created them, in causing them to turn outward" have been
substituted for "in creating them with outgoing tendencies."
64 true light that enlightens   John 1:9
64 permanent possibility of sensation   I believe that this phrase was coined
by John Stuart Mill, but have been unable to locate it. It is a definition
that calls to mind a modern hypothesis, referred to by John A. Wheeler
in a paper on the origin of the universe, that no universe is possible that
does not include the possibility of an observer.
66 The measured thunder   This poem is first published here.
72 ¶A central secret   The idea of meeting everyone on his or her own
level became further clarified for me after reading J. Allen, *Kinship with
All Life* (New York: Harper & Row, 1954).
74 I am in all created things   This poem is first published here.

THE NOW OF SPIRIT

77 Between me and the moving world's   Reprinted from *The Living Seed*,
p. 92, by permission of Harcourt Brace Jovanovich, © 1962 by John
Moffitt.
80 Across the beach of sky   Reprinted from *Escape of the Leopard*, p. 27,
by permission of Harcourt Brace Jovanovich, © 1963 by John Moffitt.
81 ¶More clearly related   The same sort of experience visits musical
composers—far more intensely, as it would seem. Haydn and Mozart
and Brahms have all spoken of their enjoying it and of its astonishing
flow; Bach and Beethoven provide convincing evidence of having known
it habitually to an extraordinary degree. It is given, of course, to many
writers and other creative artists. Malvina Hoffman, the gifted American
sculptor, told me of sometimes feeling, as she began work, as if her chisel
was being moved by a power other than her own. This is not to say that

very many works of art of all kinds are not produced through conscious application of the intellect from the start. But in my belief, at least where poems are concerned, those that one goes back to again and again for enlargement of vision embody a good portion that has not been contrived by the unaided human intellect. Interesting accounts of Brahms' and other composers' experiences may be found in Arthur M. Abell, *Talks with Great Composers* (Garmisch-Pastenkirchen, Germany: G. E. Schroeder Verlag, 1964).

inspiration Its first occurrence in my own case was when I was eight years old, at which time I wrote a poem of several stanzas (plus chorus, spelled "cours.") titled "Beautyful Flowers Birds and Bees," preserved by my parents in the original manuscript. One could hardly expect so elaborate a poem to be written by one so young. It is startling to find in my own childish handwriting, among many appropriately simple and at times playful or foolish childhood sentiments, the sudden line: "Oh, beautyful are the feet of those who walk on the pathwaws [sic] of light."

poetic trance The phrase was used by the poet Robert Graves in *The Crowning Privilege* (Garden City, N. Y.: Doubleday & Co., 1956).

83 ¶*Both in the Old Testament* For some of the details in this and the following paragraph I am indebted to Michael Schmaus, "Holy Spirit," *Sacramentum Mundi* (ref. note for p. 53 above), vol. 3, pp. 53–56.

When God began to create Genesis 1:1–2. The Hebrew text yields this translation rather than "In the beginning God created. . . ."

breath of the Almighty Job 33:4

¶*The spirit of God* Cf. 1 Samuel 10:10

84 *pour out . . . on all flesh* Joel 2:28–32; see Acts 2:16. For some of the details in this paragraph, I am indebted to Michael Schmaus, "Holy Spirit," *Sacramentum Mundi* (ref. note for p. 83 above). If one accepts Peter's view of the spirit of God, instead of pointing to the Day of Pentecost as the "beginning" of the Holy Spirit's communication to the Christian church, one might interpret it rather as the beginning of the church's *being aware* of being led by the Spirit.

84 *from the beginning* 1 John 2:13; cf. John 1:1–2

He was in the world John 1:10

God began to create See ref. note for p. 83 above.

through whom also Hebrews 1:2

true light that enlightens John 1:9 To my way of thinking, it only complicates matters to try to differentiate Christ as active creative principle and active enlightening principle from the spirit of God or the Holy Spirit. Where Jesus tells the disciples, "When the Spirit of truth comes, he will guide you into all the truth" (John 16:13; see also John 14:16–17), we may be allowed to see this as promising his own continued presence and working throughout all subsequent human history. Moreover, the intervention of the Spirit through the gifts of prophecy and inspiration (whether in the past or the future) is hard to differentiate from Christ's own working. Both Peter and Paul appear to equate the terms "Spirit of God" and "Spirit of Christ" (see Romans 8:9; 1 Peter 1:11). These terms appear to be closely related to Jesus' term "Spirit of truth."

85 *Truly, truly, I say*   John 8:58
  Lo, I am with you   Matthew 28:20
  timeless Christ   See *Journey to Gorakhpur* (ref. note for p. 49 above), p. 269ff.
  Author of life   Acts 3:15
  In him was life   John 1:4
  he reflects the glory   Hebrews 1:3
  not far from each one   Acts 17:27
  hidden for ages   Colossians 1:26
  Christ in you   Colossians 1:27

86 *Presence*   The poem appears on p. 77.
  being and becoming   The phrase is derived from Vivekananda, but I have been unable to locate it.

87 *This Atman is Brahman*   *Mandukya Upanishad* 2; *Brihadaranyaka Upanishad* 4.4.5
  ¶*What then is Brahman?*   The description of Brahman as Being-Awareness-Joy Absolute (the Sanskrit *Sachchidananda* is composed of the three terms *Sat, Chit,* and *Ananda*), though implicit in the earliest Upanishads, is not found there. It occurs only in a few minor (and later) Upanishadic texts, such as *Maitrayani Upanishad* 3.12; *Nrisimhauttaratapini Upanishad* 6,7; *Ramapurvatapini Upanishad* 5.8; *Ramauttaratapini Upanishad* 2, as mentioned by Swami Nikhilananda in *The Upanishads,* vol. 1 (Harper & Bros., 1949), p. 36n.

88 *Now, therefore, the description*   *Brihadaranyaka Upanishad* 2.3.6
  Through what should one know   Ibid. 2.4.14
  Brahman without attributes   The Sanskrit term is *Nirguna Brahman.*
  Now the designation   *Brihadaranyaka Upanishad* 2.3.6
  It shines through the functions   Bhagavad Gita 13.14–17. Quotations from this scripture are taken from Swami Nikhilananda (trans.), *The Bhagavad Gita* (Ramakrishna-Vivekananda Center, 1944), and occasionally adapted for poetical reasons or for the sake of clarity. In line 4 of this quotation, the word "qualities" has been substituted for the Sanskrit *gunas* in the original translation.
  ¶*The Godhead is here*   The mystic enjoying this direct experience is referred to by the great nineteenth-century Hindu saint Ramakrishna as a *vijnani,* or mature mystic. For references to the *vijnani,* see Swami Nikhilananda (trans.), *The Gospel of Sri Ramakrishna* (New York: Rama-krishna-Vivekananda Center, 1942), pp. 852, 911.

89 *Atman, smaller than the small*   Katha Upanishad 1.2.20
  Though sitting still   Ibid. 1.2.21
  It is never born   Bhagavad Gita 2.20
  It is through Atman   Katha Upanishad 2.1.3–4

89 ¶As we noted   See first ref. note for p. 87.

¶*Krishna, both through his*   For more about the "descent" of Vishnu, see Bhagavad Gita 4.6–8.

90 He who sees me everywhere   Bhagavad Gita 6.30–32

  Abode of Brahman   Ibid. 14.27

  Earth, water, fire   Ibid. 7.4–7, 10. In the Sanskrit, in place of the words "O Arjuna," where they occur the second and third times in this quotation, the words "O Dhananjaya" and "O son of Pritha" (both epithets of Arjuna) are used.

93 It all seemed a strange language   This poem is first published here.

95 The unique advantage of seeing   First published here.

96 I walk in a music   First published here.

  Every thing and every person   First published here.

97 pearl of great price   Matthew 13:46

  ¶*Obviously the experience*   For a discussion of the five "elements" of the sense-perceived world mentioned near the end of this paragraph, see Swami Nikhilananda (trans.), *The Bhagavad Gita* (ref. note for p. 88 above), 7.4, pp. 180–181.

105 all things were created   Colossians 1:17

  it is no longer I   Galatians 2:30

106 Light even of lights   Bhagavad Gita 13.17; see also *Mundaka Upanishad* 2.2.9.

106 was moving over the face   Genesis 1:2

107 cause and effect   It may be noted here that the Buddha's principle of "dependent origination" or "conditioned genesis," which was revealed in one of the stages of his illumination, may itself be taken as another name for the working of spirit. For a discussion of this principle, see Walpola Rahula, *What the Buddha Taught* (New York: Grove Press, 1974), p. 53.

The term "Now," used in the last sentence of this paragraph and occasionally throughout the book, and the term "Now of Spirit," also frequently used, are to be subtly distinguished. What is meant by "Now" is this same pervadingly creative Now of Spirit when intuitively experienced *without reference* to sun or self or spirit as separate entities. It is spirit as it is given to us to experience it from moment to moment in daily life—once we have learned how to open ourselves to it fully (and as we already experience it in our best moments of attentiveness).

108 Dare I divide   From *This Narrow World* (New York: Dodd, Mead & Company, 1958), p. 47.

THE ROAD TO NOW

111 To walk expertly   This poem is first published here.

112 crux of now   See the poem "Presence" on p. 77.

113 involved   See Swami Vivekananda, "The Cosmos: The Macrocosm," *Vivekananda: The Yogas and Other Works* (ref. note for p. 44 above), pp. 290–291.

116 ¶The immediate source   For some of the details in this paragraph I am indebted to Heinz Haber, *Stars, Men, and Atoms* and Kenneth Weaver, "The Incredible Universe," *National Geographic Magazine* (ref. note for p. 22 above).

117 Dawn breaks where sundown was   From *Signal Message* (The Golden Quill Press, 1982), p. 76.

124 The watcher at the spring   Reprinted from *Escape of the Leopard,* p. 61, by permission of Harcourt Brace Jovanovich, © 1966 by John Moffitt.

125 ¶At midday   For the source of a few of the details in this paragraph see ref. note for p. 116 above. The figures for the sun's mass were obtained from the entry "Sun," *Encyclopedia of Science and Technology* (New York: McGraw-Hill Book Co., 1977), pp. 275–296.

132 ¶We noted earlier   An arresting hint of what such full attentiveness means, in actual experience, is to be found in a line from a poem by an ancient Zen master: "To forget myself is to be testified to by everything in the world." It is quoted from Zenkei Shibayama, *Zen Comments on the Mumonkan* (New York: Harper & Row, 1974), p. 310 (used by permission). The "myself" here referred to is the ego-self. Another Zen saying gives further insight into this one: "Actually, the seer to see into is the seen to be seen into" (ibid., p. 324).

132 To see them as they are would be   Reprinted from *Escape of the Leopard,* p. 66, by permission of Harcourt Brace Jovanovich, © 1974 by John Moffitt.

135 Know: I depend on no one   See Swami Atmaghanananda, "Further Light on Vivekananda's Inspired Talks," *Vedanta Kesari* (September 1963), p. 363. The statement should not be taken to suggest that the grace of God (or of the Self) is not necessary for success.

¶We can encourage   Two excellent works for encouraging openness to spirit are J. P. de Caussade, *Self-Abandonment to Divine Providence* (London: Burns Oates & Washbourne, 1953) and Susanna Winkworth (trans.), *Theologia Germanica* (New York: The Macmillan Co., 1901).

136 from within   From Zenkei Shibayama, *Zen Comments on the Mumonkan* (ref. note for p. 132 above), p. 199 (used by permission): "It is an ironclad rule in Zen always to read the teaching, however it may be expressed, from within, based on the experiential fact, and never try to reach the experiential fact by following any particular form of expression." My own ideas about reading spiritual teachings were made clearer by this sentence.

138 The pride of a saint   From *Sayings of Sri Ramakrishna* (Madras: Sri Ramakrishna Math, 1960), p. 54 (translation adapted).

EPILOGUE

139 goings-on of the universe   From the Preface to the second edition of William Wordsworth's *Lyrical Ballads*. See *Wordsworth's Poetical Works* (London: Oxford University Press, 1926), p. 937.

141 ¶It is this fact   The intuition that *we* know reality suggests that the noumenal world is not "real" to us in any meaningful sense except as it is revealed in physical phenomena and in the person; that the world we have been perceiving all along, and the senses and mind we have been perceiving it with are, when read from within, all we need to know; that an "ultimate" reality that is really transcendent or wholly other is an abstraction, necessary no doubt for rigorous thinking but in no way available to human experience, and so far as we are concerned totally dependent for its existence on our own powers of inference. When Sigmund Freud pointed out the inaccessibility to consciousness of the realm of the unconscious, did his words not hint at the fact that our business—so long as we are healthy in mind—is with the realm of the conscious? How much more so, then, when it comes to an inaccessible noumenal world. To insist that ultimate reality is somewhere else than "here" (a here irradiated, perhaps by other areas of existence unavailable to conscious thought) is to cut at the root of all normal human assumptions and even of the now-and-here reality of the one making the assertion.

142 ¶Our aim throughout   In a certain sense our diagram of a threefold environment—a world of sun, world of self, and world of spirit—is devised simply for the sake of intellectual understanding. To discuss any of these elements intelligently we have to abstract them from the four-dimensional reality of direct experience of which they are component parts. In that sense they may seem to be less real than the total experience itself. Yet even then, common sense tells us, they *are* somehow separate realities, too. And once we no longer confuse the self with the flow of distracting ego-thoughts that constitutes the ego-self, once we have known everything as the working of spirit, all doubt ceases. All three worlds are seen to have their legitimate place—their "difference in identity" as certain Hindus would say—in the never-ending discourse that is our Now; and so, of course, do intellect and emotion and intuition, as "separate" entities.

143 devouring fire   Exodus 24:17

The thought that things beyond immediate perception or conception are "more basic" than our surface world has no meaning, even as hypothesis, unless it achieves reality on the *surface* of the mind, through the working of spirit. It can in no way dispute the prime importance of the surface world in space-time that it seeks to explain away, except in its abstract three-dimensional world.

shine before men   Matthew 5:16

For there is nothing hid   Mark 4:22; cf. Matthew 5:15, Luke 11:33

If any man has ears   Mark 4:23
true light that enlightens   John 1:9
143 *your light . . . shine before men*   Matthew 5:16
145 *Do you know the hour*   This poem is first published here.

APPENDIX A

148 ¶*Once the mind is*   I have freely adapted this daily meditative exercise from one used in his meditation classes by the late Swami Nikhilananda, who derived it, to the best of my knowledge, from an exercise composed for students in America in the first decade of the twentieth century by Swami Saradananda, an important disciple of Ramakrishna.
152 *I meditate on the glory*   For the literal translation of the Gayatri Mantra, see p. 17. It is customary in modern India to add as a prefix to the mantra (which is to say, sacred Sanskrit text) the Sanskrit words *Om. Bhuh Buvah Swah* ("Om. Earth, heaven, the spaces between"). A freer translation of the whole is:

> Om. We meditate on that unparalleled resplendent Being who energizes the sun and pervades earth, heaven, and the spaces between. May he illumine our understanding.

("Om" is, in Hindu belief, the eternal Word, the first manifested sound; it is a symbol both of the personal God and of the suprapersonal Godhead.)

APPENDIX C

159 *Samadhi . . . is only*   Cf. the chapter "Vivekananda" from *Vivekananda: the Yogas and Other Works* (ref. note for p. 44 above), pp. 30–31. I have been unable to locate the exact quotation given here.
160 ¶ *It may also be observed*   One striking illustration of this sort of person is the late Clara Sipprell, the gifted photographer, whom I was privileged to know. Of all the persons I have met, she possessed the quality of positive attentiveness to an exceptional degree. Whenever I talked with her, I felt I was receiving her complete attention, and presumably she gave that same attention to whatever she undertook to accomplish. She exhibited also a rare balance of mind and what appeared to be almost complete selflessness. A lifelong friend of hers has reported that she was so wonderful a receiver that she gave the most intense pleasure to anyone who did something for her, however insignificant. These qualities in her were apparent from a young age; they seem not to have been acquired with the help of conscious discipline.